ETERNITY INVADING TIME

ETERNITY INVADING TIME

Advantage
BOOKS

Renny McLean

Eternity Invading Time by Renny McLean
Copyright © 2005 by Renwick G. McLean
All Rights Reserved
ISBN: 978-1-59755-705-4
Published by: ADVANTAGE BOOKS™
                 Longwood, FL
                 www.advbookstore.com

All Scripture quotations, unless otherwise noted are taken from The Holy Bible, Authorized King James Version. Public Domain

Scripture quotations marked NIV taken from the Holy Bible, New International Version® NIV®. Copyright ©1973, 1978, 1984, 2011 by Biblica, Inc©. Used by permission of Biblica, Inc©. All rights reserved worldwide.

Scripture quotations marked NKJV are taken from the NEW KING JAMES VERSION®. Copyright© 1982 by Thomas Nelson, Inc. Used by permission. All rights reserved.

Scripture quotations marked Youngs Translation are taken from the 1898 Young's Literal Translation of the Holy Bible by J.N. Young, public domain.

Scripture quotations marked Weymouth Translation are taken from the New Testament In Modern Speech by Richard Francis Weymouth, published in 1903; public domain

LIBRARY OF CONGRESS CONTROL NUMBER: 2005929089
SUBJECTS: RELIGION: Christian Life – Inspirational

9th Printing: July 2021
21 22 23 24 25 26 15 14 13 12 11 10 9

Table of Contents

~Forewords~

We are truly living in momentous times. This is an exciting time to be alive but, more exciting for the person who has by faith reached forth toward eternity and has begun to bring eternity into the present.

The Bible tells us that in the end times *"...Knowledge shall be increased": Daniel 12:4*. We see that today there is great knowledge available to all of us as never before. The scientific developments are tremendous. The medical world has opened up new ways of helping us to live. The business world has brought new developments, new ideas, new inventions, greater, larger, and finer ways to travel, live and enjoy life.

If that is true in the natural, and it is, then we must grasp hold of the fact that it is also true in the spiritual. God, by revelation is helping us to comprehend the great truths He has given to us through His Word. This is not a new "Gospel"; this manuscript helps us by revelation and faith to move into the realm of the "Spirit" so that we can better "understand the things that God has declared."

This book will help you to realize that you can move beyond anything you have experienced in your Christian walk. It will bring you face to face with the eternal truths of God. Let God be God! Let your faith move up another step and begin to experience the great things that God has promised you.

Bishop, Elder, Dr. R. G. McLean has not just written another book, he has shared with us the revelation of God's truth that has challenged and changed his life and moved him into a world wide supernatural ministry.

Let God touch your heart through the reading of this revelation of truth.

S. K. Biffle
CFO Full Gospel Fellowship of Churches and Ministers Int.

****

It is an honor to write an foreword for this book of Faith by Dr. Renny McLean. I have known Dr. McLean for years and I have listened to many of his tapes. He travels around the world sharing the Gospel of Christ with those who are in need of the Word. He preaches to thousands of people in crusades in Asia, Africa, Europe and India, as well as in the United States. Dr. McLean is one of the foremost authorities on Faith in the Word of God. It is a real privilege to work as his Bishop and watch the Spirit move in his ministry. Enjoy this book as you read, and let Faith come to life and manifest itself within you!

Bishop C.W. Goforth
Florida District Pentecostal Church of God
Assistant General Bishop Pentecostal Church of God

∼ In Dedication ∼

This book is dedicated to The Father, The Son and The Holy Spirit for their exquisite counsel and tutelage of those of us He calls son and daughter.

To the end time Body of Christ, to those who have been called and equipped for such a time as this, to reveal the Glory of God on the earth.

To the Apostles, Prophets, Evangelists, Pastors and Teachers, past, present and future, who laid foundation stones for us all.

And to you, the reader, may your journey on the earth never cease until you stand before God, where time is no more, and your joy is unspeakable and full of Glory!

Renny McLean

~ Acknowledgments ~

I could not have accomplished this book had it not been for my wife, Marina and my children, Maranatha, Caleb and Zoe. Thank you for being so patient and supportive.

My parents, George and Mavis McLean; my in-laws, the late Charles Headlam and Clarice Headlam; and my brothers and sisters, Kathleen, Angela, Paul, Rose, Patricia, and Wendy; the late Florence Hines who gave me my Jewish heritage; I love each one of you deeply.

I want to thank God that I had the privilege of being raised in Great Britain. The metropolitan melting pot served me well. I was to learn how to appreciate the many diverse cultures as they crisscrossed through London before moving to Dallas, Texas.

To our Global Glory family, there are not enough words to express how I feel about your love, support and prayers.

And to the rest of the Global Glory team, especially our spiritual covering of Rev. C.W. Goforth and the Pentecostal Church of God, Rev. Al and Dr. Billie Deck, Chris Kennedy, Kevin Forney, Rev. Josh and Iffy Nathan.

To Dr. Don Arnold and Dr. Bud Biffle; as well as the entire Full Gospel Fellowship of Churches and Ministries, Jerry and Lucretia Hobbs, Mike and Margaret Maxey, Ken and Faith Shipp, Joyce Essman in the editing of this book.

And a special thanks to all the instructors at Global Glory Institute, Rev. David Alleredge, who has been a great help in the editing of this work, Rev. John and Emma Stewart, Pastor Tony and Debbie Davidson, Jo Martin, Isaac and Sally Williams, Sue Gilpin, Billy and Cynthia Thompson, Rev. Barrington and Maxine Burrell, Bishop Keith and Winnie McCloud, Rev. Gordon & Louise Young, Ron and Beverly Prestage, Bill and Connie Wilson and Mother Jenkins, Pastor Paul and Kathy Melnichuk and The Toronto Prayer Palace.

Emma Butler, Bob and Sharon Koons, Ruth Meadows, Rev. Ervin and the late Mabel Smith, and Rev. Ademas.

I would be remiss if I did not mention the late Ruth Ward Heflin, Benny Hinn, Dr. Morris Cerullo, Dr. T.L. Osborn, and to the thousands of our sons and daughters around the world. May God bless each one of you for your investment in my life and ministry. There are countless people who have opened doors for our ministry around the world, and to each and everyone of you, I want to express my heartfelt thanks.

And to God, The Creator of all things seen and unseen. To The Father, The Son, and The Holy Spirit, for without Him was nothing made that was made, even me. Lord, you are my Sovereign King, my Prince of Peace, my Everlasting Father and the Salvation of my soul. Praise-a-lujah! For our names are listed in the Lamb's Book of Life.

- Dr. R. G. McLean

~ Introduction ~

Dr. R.G. McLean has been asked what Bible college and seminary did you attend and how long did you study there? Where did you learn the vernacular to describe the undiscerned things that you are able to express so graphically?

My usual reply is, "I studied at Calvary. My seminary was at the feet of the Lord. My vocabulary is from the angels bringing me the revelation in the early years and from my visitation to the heavens in my later years."

Those early encounters captured my passion to the point where nothing else mattered other than entering into and staying in the Glory of God. My dedication became the presence of the Lord and that He would establish my lifestyle. My lifestyle became a discipline of prayer, fasting and worship.

Before you read this book, I want to advise you that you will understand the Creator with renewed understanding. The Webster dictionary describes the word 'God' as: "the ruler of the universe, regarded as eternal infinite, all-powerful, Supreme Being Almighty."

The church finds the word "supernatural" or "supreme ruler" an awkward phrase to describe God. Yet science fiction, government and religious organizations can set the boundaries for what is considered normal or supernatural. The media has successfully desensitized us from the awesome power of God.

I challenge the believer to redefine their understanding of the basic truth of their walk with God. I describe faith as an antenna whose frequency is being tuned to the spiritual waves that come directly from the throne. Faith is also a currency of heaven. You need faith to see God, to trade with God at His level, and to withdraw from the resources of glory. It is only through faith the mind can conceive that the world was framed from the invisible principles that the Father has to reveal. Science cannot reason away faith; neither can it explain it.

The devil's job is to keep you focused at what you can see versus what already exists in the realm of the Spirit. Consequently, you are reduced to believing only what you see. Religion has also played a large part in your unbelief. Religion keeps you bound to your past, denying your present and delaying your future. Subsequently you have no basis for your faith to be built upon the Word of God.

Many of you will look at the title of this book, *Eternity Invading Time*, and ask what this is all about! Time is Eternity's child, eternity was before time, and time was set in creation on the fourth day. God set the sun to rule by day and the moon to rule by night, thereby establishing time and season.

Through the pages of this book you will understand that time is aligning itself to the eternal purposes that were set before the foundations of the world. The Bible declares that the Lamb was slain before the foundations of the world. However, it took time— four thousand years—to see the drama played out through Jesus.

You will be challenged to speak from the eternal realm into time. You will learn the principles that will help you to activate miracles in your ministry. You cannot see miracles by applying natural time frame. You will lose the manifestation of a miracle every time. Every thing in the eternal realm has already happened. Miracles have already taken place. Missing body parts, financial, emotional and relational needs have already been met. You have to call it from the realm in which it already exists into the realm in which it will manifest.

I spoke about seeing new worlds being created on one of my visitation to the heavens. I saw new stars being created by the power of God, just for His pleasure. I saw universes that I could not fathom where they would fit in our stratosphere. Yet Time Magazine and the NASA telescope are always verifying new planets and stars beyond our galaxy. I don't wait for science to confirm what I have seen in the heavens as my reality; I visit the heavens to see the reality from which I was created.

You are beginning a great journey; your appetite will be ignited with passion for the presence of the Creator. You will visit the secret chambers of the Father to worship Him and receive the mysteries from Him face to face. You will view science in a brand new way. Science will not be giving you reasoning and theories to base your understanding; it will be revelation knowledge that will give you the definition of the unseen realm. Your life and ministry will take on the characteristics of the heavens. Heaven's vocabulary will become yours. Today sit back, take your shoes off, take your watches off, turn down your clocks. Time is about to be invaded by the eternal destiny of God. Praise-A-Lu-Jah!

CHAPTER ONE

My Life as a Child

"Geniuses and prophets usually do not excel in professional learning, and their originality, if any, is often due precisely to the fact that they do not."
-J.A. Schumpeter

Once upon a time, in a place where time was not, a called out to a created being. The being was instructed that it had a destiny, and that the predetermined plan for it was beginning. And by the miracle of the spoken Word of it's Creator, the being came out of the eternal. It was in this eternal realm where His Creator had foreknowledge of the being. That being was given a name not known to man or itself, and then was placed into the seed of a man on the earth. The man met the woman who was destined to carry the seed to full term, and they jointly created a being of destiny. That being of destiny was me. I am now on a time leased appointment with His destiny for my life. But, not everything began as simple as these first few lines.

I have never been a student who had a great deal of interest in the findings of man. While I was growing up in London, I found myself drawn to the things of God in such a manner that my teachers thought I was daydreaming. I guess there was a little truth to that, but I was not dreaming about not being in the classroom. I was reliving the experiences I had been having since childhood. These events were so powerful that they left the common things of the classroom a bit boring. Dreamers live in the hereafter, even though they live in the here and now.

The Spirit of God began to unveil the truths tucked away in the Word of God. I was made to understand those things that I had no training to understand. I was able to grasp eternal concepts which to others were complicated and confusing. As the years progressed, I would come to have a working knowledge of the Word, and heart, of God. The revelatory realm became more real to me than the reality I was living in. The nations of the world became the heartbeat inside me.

I have had the privilege of teaching in a number of Bible schools, and every one of them asked me, "What graduate school did you attend?" I simply answered them with the best answer I could give them, "I was taught in the graduate class in the Glory realm of God." The look on their faces told the story. They just could not understand what I was saying to them. Some of them thought I was being what we might consider a bit high-minded, arrogant or egotistical, when that was just not the case. Finally, I would have to share with them what I meant. After I would explain, the students would then begin to ask me questions, and I was thrilled to share what had been given to me by the Spirit of God to those hungry hearts. I trust your heart is hungry to know Him and the wonderful array of truths and revelations He has prepared for all of His children. I pray that you will find Him to be as exciting as I have. This great Creator is more than I can even begin to share with you. But as I can, I will. My story is not so unusual. There are many who have had similar experiences as I have and have been used by God. It is just that I am here for such a time as this to share my beginnings with you, as well as those things I have learned through those precious moments I spent in His presence.

You see, I have been to Heaven on several occasions, Scripturally referred to as being "caught up in the Spirit". For some of you this comment will have a profound effect, while on others it will cause you to wonder about the comments I will make in this book. So, let us agree from the start that I will tell my story with an honest heart, without guile or manipulation. This will be a telling of what has happened to me, and how I experienced it. The occasional reference I might make to a miracle in one of the services will be accurate and verifiable. This is not a book to make you stand in awe of me. This is a book which, I sincerely pray, will leave you in awe of Him. And if I am coming to you with an open heart, I would ask that you read with an open mind, and do not judge me by any measure, for what has happened to me is my testimonial as to what I have witnessed.

So let us begin with a few basic bits of information. I was saved at age five, and it was at that time that I had my first encounter with the manifest presence of the Lord.

When I was seven, I had a supernatural experience that changed my life. I remember it like it was yesterday. I was preparing to go to bed, and as usual I would always pray, "Praise the Lord. Hallelujah! Thank you, Lord, for today. Thank You for health and strength. Thank you for Mommy. Thank you for Daddy. Thank you for all my brothers and sisters. I love you, Lord".

As soon as I pulled the blanket over my head, a light came in my room that wasn't the result of electricity. Out of the light, came the person of Jesus. I saw the entrance to Heaven, and He looked at me and called to me to come to Him. Suddenly, the light He came out of engulfed the entire room. Suddenly I was aware that I was not in my room. The walls had vanished, there was no ceiling, just the light of His Glory filling every direction I looked.

****

"Colors in Heaven were alive, radiating the presence of God."

****

I saw the angelic beings going around His throne in worship. I saw a rainbow around the throne in living color. Somehow, I understood that colors in Heaven were alive, radiating the presence of God. I was aware that the colors in Heaven were responding to a sound. As I continued to observe what was happening, I became aware that the worship around the throne was affecting the colors in the rainbow, and the colors surrounded His throne.

As the Lord continued to speak to me, he began to show me things which I have never forgotten to this day. I saw life as He sees it. It was completely different from what we would consider life. There are no words to explain what I observed. You must remember, I was a child, with a child's understanding. I would come to understand the things I saw with greater clarity as I grew older. Then I was taken to where time began. I saw moments in time where things happened on the earth that had prophetic importance. Even at that young age, I somehow understood the concept of eternity invading time. It was easy for me to see that time was a created event.

My dear reader, time is eternity's child. It is the offspring of the eternal design. Time could not, will not, or cannot be greater than the eternal. Sometimes we make the mistake of looking to time for the answer. There is an old saying that time heals all wounds. The truth is that time does not possess the power to do anything. It is an illusion. That which time was birthed from holds the answer. The eternal was the womb from which time came from. It was a product of His design. The original must be there before any replication, of any part of it, can be manufactured.

When the physical presence of Jesus came into my room, He stood before me at the end of my bed. Two beautiful angelic beings stood by His side.

He said to me, *"I have called you to preach. You will say things that are native to the throne. You will not be taught by man, nor will your mind be fashioned like most men. You will be fashioned by Me. I will deal with you according to the seasons of your life. I have called you to go to the nations."*

When He said the word "nations," a globe emerged out from His mouth. I saw Heavenly stars hovering over every place I was to preach. I could see every nation that I would later be going into to minister for Him. When I went to the nations later in my life, it felt so natural for me to be there because I had been there in the Spirit as a child.

By the time I was twelve, I was preaching. I don't mean reading a Scripture in a service. I was standing in the pulpit and preaching. It came as easily to me then as it does today. He was fashioning me by His hand.

In one of the times, I was sitting before Him, the Lord said, *"The revelation that I will put in your Spirit will take you past what you've been used to all your life. In the latter years before I return, I will use you to bring the revelations of the Heavens to my people."*

I remember telling my mother about my visions, and she thought I was a bit crazy at the time. The people in the Pentecostal Church where I was raised were not comfortable with a child having the kind of ministry, I had at such a young age. They were more fearful of the gift than to see it for what it was. Instead of acknowledging His presence and exclaiming their joy that God had chosen to lay His hand on one so young, they were judgmental and closed-minded. I would learn in my later years that this was nothing more than the religious spirit of that denomination. They felt that because there were so many manifestations happening around me that something was wrong. I was not doing anything but just speaking out of my heart, and the manifestations were just happening.

I knew that the Lord was in charge of my life, and nothing that anyone said would change my mind, or what I was doing for Him. I have been deliberately faithful to the charge He gave me in those words. I love the church with a deep passion, and I am fully aware that you cannot live in the excitement of manifestations, no matter how great they may be. But we must have revelation before we can have manifestation. You cannot get fire out of water! It takes a fire to set a fire. It takes a certain amount of rain to cause a flood. Without a constant flow of revelation, manifestations will not tarry. It is expedient that we have revelation. I'm not talking about doctrine. If doctrine could have brought revival, we would be in the greatest revival the world has ever seen by now.

Without a doubt, I was destined to preach a Rhema word to the household of faith. Someone asked me why miracles happen with such ease in our meetings. My answer was, "The seventh day is a day of rest. Since I am resting in Him, I don't do it. God is the one who's doing it. I don't make miracles happen, He does!" I came to a realization at a young age that faith is the ever-empowering awareness of the invisible world and its realities.

Miracles happen at the appointed time God planned for them to happen. He already planned that from the very beginning of time.

The best is yet to come! We are at a critical time in the history of the planet earth. Right now, there is nothing taking place on the earth void of spiritual significance. Each and every event has such powerful reasons for them taking place, it is often hard to perceive the divine purpose in them. Political, educational, cultural, sociological and economical arenas are being shaken. The wars which are raging all over the world are mere fulfillment of the prophetic Scriptures which heralded their arrivals. Right now everything is happening according to God's plan. Remember, as great as the church is, and was, there is still more to come. Despite all the moves of God we've experienced, the best is yet to come. There has to be something greater than what we've experienced up until now. Still, millions of people are outside the kingdom of God. There are sicknesses in the church today that haven't been healed, and diseases which are yet to be cured. What will it take to awaken us that what we have been doing for all these years is not working? We must change the course we are on. We must rethink how we interact with the Word of God, not to mention His presence.

We have witnessed tremendous things but, as great as those things were, we must see beyond them. We must look beyond what we see even now. We must look to where He is now. We must press on and pursue those greater things of God. He told us in His Word that we would do greater things than He did. If you look at the simple fact that we move around the globe at a faster rate of

17

speed to carry His message to the nations, that in itself is one way we are doing things greater than He did. When the Apostle Paul would send a letter to one of the churches they would gather together, and with parchment and quill in hand, to copy down the words as they were read to the church. I cannot begin to count how many versions of the Bible I have in my library—that is doing greater than.... When I see all the wonderful Christian programming which is aired I am once again reminded that this too is a greater than situation.

While Jesus and the disciples were limited in their scope of influence to a smaller geographical setting, the impact of what they accomplished was multiplied millions of times over as the message reached out to the world. There was a time when the known world considered themselves as Christian. Today, with all the technological advances in communication, we have access to the world via the Internet, not to mention television and radio. Our geographical location is no more important than it was in those days. The content of the message, or should I say the power in the message, is what takes the information and distributes it to the masses.

I thank God for everything I have witnessed. All the miracles, wonders, signs, manifestations, the glorious and the marvelous acts have always been as exciting for me to behold as those who attended the services. Since I am not doing them, I get as excited to see what He will do as the next person. I have asked God for many things. One of them is the salvation of my family. I still have family members who are not saved. They've even been to my meetings and seen with their own eyes all kinds of wonders and miracles performed by God, but they are still not saved. But I am continuing to stand on the Word of God where He promises that your whole house would be saved, delivered and set free.

In Acts 16:31, it reads: "And they said, Believe on the Lord Jesus Christ, and thou shalt be saved, and thy house."

I am so grateful to the Lord for the fact that my children are serving the Lord. Maranatha, Caleb and Zoe are all brilliant children. They help in the ministry office during the year in so many different ways. They never cease to amaze me as to their concepts of the world they live in. Living here in the United States has given them a completely different take on the things from their early years in London. To say they have become Americanized would be an improper statement. They are global children, with a global view most of us have not been raised with. I do not have the foggiest idea as to how to operate a computer, but they know all about them. They seem to thrive in the technology world. At least I have conquered my cell phone!

If you knew me as well as some, you would find that I still have that same childlike fascination when it comes to the Glory realm of God. I am fascinated by how it interacts with us, how it is the glue that holds everything together. The Glory of God still amazes me. To have been to Heaven, walked the streets of gold, stood in the throne room, talked to the angels and to have been instructed while in the manifest presence of the Lord has left a stamp on my spirit which nothing can remove. Some people have asked why I have not shared all the things I have seen in those Heavenly visits. There is a very simple answer to that question. It is not the time for those things to be revealed. There are times when I feel like the Prophet Daniel, John the Revelator and Paul the Apostle, who were instructed that there were things they could not share until an appointed time. Once again, we see that word "time." While it has no effect on the eternal, it serves that which is prophetic.

I was given a very powerful command to begin to share more than I have ever shared in the past. And as He releases me to share these revelations, you will hear them and read them in print. Some of you will have to truly seek understanding as you read this book.

The concepts are not natural to the mind of man. There are phrases which are not part of the vocabulary of modern man. And as you encounter them, do not fear or fight them. They are nothing more than millennial concepts for such a time as this. What you are hearing is His vocabulary. Those who have an ear to hear, let them hear what the Spirit is saying to the church at this time. We are being given instructions which will determine our role in these last days.

You must learn His voiceprint. It is imperative that you know Him as He knows you from the eternal. You are that individual He had foreknowledge of. He knows the plans He has for you, and they are for you to prosper, and to give you a future! Allow your understanding to wrap around His promises.

The God of the universe has always had you in His master plan. That is enough to make every man, woman, boy and girl, lift their voices to the Heavens and declare the wonders of God.

Lord of Glory! You are worthy of all the praise!

Renny McLean

CHAPTER TWO

The Creation of Time

"The planets in their stations listening stood
While the brightest pomp ascended jubilant
Open, ye everlasting gates, they sung
Open ye heavens, your living doors; let in
The great Creator from his work returned
Magnificent, His six day's work, a world."
-Milton

What is this great mystery of the first seven days of creation? The agnostic, atheistic and scientific mind says there must have been some big bang which caused all life forms to come into existence. Well, there was a loud noise all right, just not the kind they are talking about. The loud noise heard was the voice of the Almighty penetrating the vastness of His perception in the eternal realm as He spoke into existence that which He had already created within His being. All He had to do was to call out of Himself those things which were a part of His Glory, and they would respond.

The truly exciting part of His creation is that He took the time on the seventh day to rest! This understanding of how He created out of Himself all things may prove to be one of the greatest keys to manifesting spiritual revelation you will ever learn as you read through this book.

There are three elements which are needed for this journey, faith, imagination, and vision. You must read this book in the realm of faith. Without it, you will not hear what the Spirit is saying. Imagination is one of the characteristics of the creative side of God. He imagined those things He created, then spoke them into being. You must rely on the DNA of the Almighty which resides in you. To see into the invisible realm of the supernatural you must have vision.

Without vision you will perish in the midst of some of the most thought-provoking moments you have ever experienced. You will be required to visualize and perceive the realms of God as well as the concepts therein.

You are now invited to pull back the curtain on that event called creation. You have an armchair seat, and a written invitation from the King of Kings, to watch and see that the Lord is good, and His mercies endure forever! The creation you see is the evidence and proof positive that God has spoken.

"And God said, Let there be lights in the firmament of the heaven to divide the day from the night; and let them be for signs, and for seasons, and for days, and years: And let them be for lights in the firmament of the heaven to give light upon the earth: and it was so. And God made two great lights; the greater light to rule the day, and the lesser light to rule the night: he made the stars also. And God set them in the firmament of the heaven to give light upon the earth, And to rule over the day and over the night, and to divide the light from the darkness: and God saw that it was good." (Genesis 1:14-18)

What an incredible display of the creative power of God this series of events must have been. Imagine God the Father, God the Son (Jesus Christ), and the Holy Spirit in the Heavenly city. As they look far away, they observe a sphere without beauty, without life-giving atmosphere, void of life, much like a lump of clay waiting for the sculptor to place his hands on it. All that can be seen is a mass suspended in space.

From our armchair view we ask the question, "What is He going to do with this formless mass? What is the purpose in all this? What is my role in this eternal drama?" We may not be privy to the innermost thoughts of our Heavenly Father, but we can read the account in Genesis and visualize the mystery of the universe before our own mind's eyes.

In the beginning there were no laws regulating time, seasons, situations and circumstances, for these things did not actually exist yet. In the beginning there was only the now. Out of the mouth of God would come His expressed will and desires. Each verbal issue from His lips was met with obedience as matter and substance were divinely declared, and then controlled. The very essence of His thought life was thrust into existence and seen when He spoke. Thoughts became words, words became objective reality.

Everything was subject to the intent of His heart. The sound of His voice preceded the visible manifestation of each creative work. He said "let there be light" and there was light. Please note that the sound of His voice preceded the manifestation. This truth will carry much impact as you progress through this book. Sound precedes sight.

Western man has become saddled with the concept of setting and achieving goals. We go to sleep at night, set the alarm, and the next morning the alarm goes off and it is time to get up. The rest of the day we look at our watches to see what time it is. Time for our coffee break, time for lunch, time for ending the workday. Then we watch the clock so we can make certain we catch the evening news and weather.

****

"Time is not an absolute because it only exists when its parameters are defined by absolutes."

****

After dinner, we come to a stopping off place, and we call it a day and go to bed. The next morning the alarm goes off and we start the day all over again. We never think about the little hands going around the face of the clock, measuring out time. For most of us, time is nothing more than a measuring device we plan our day around, or the parameter within which things are accomplished.

For instance, how many times have you heard someone say, "I wish I had more time", "You're wasting time", "If I can find the time"? All are acceptable phrases. Each one denotes an intent upon time, while each phrase is impossible to fulfill. One cannot find more time, waste it or lose it.

Time is not an absolute because it only exists when its parameters are defined by absolutes. And those absolutes exist by, and through, that which God has spoken and created. It is as elusive as the wind. Take a look at your wristwatch. See how the second hand moves along effortlessly. As each movement sweeps the hand along, time is slowly evaporating into thin air. But you cannot see it leaving or disappearing. It simply slips away, never to be reclaimed. Even if you were to reset the watch back one hour it would have no effect on time. That hour is gone. As long as it took you to read the last few paragraphs, time, as you know it has silently slipped away. The last few moments will never be captured again.

This present universe is only one element of the Kingdom of God. But it is a very wonderful and important one. It is totally ludicrous for us to think that any one book can begin to reveal the intricate mechanisms of the how, and why, of the plans and purposes of God. So let us take hold of the next few moments and let us look at this phenomenon called time. Time was created, just as we were created. Time was defined by God, just as He defined us. We, along with time, did not always exist. He created it all.

Time is the product of a concept through which scientific conclusions relative to the revolving of the earth around the sun, and the revolving of the moon around the earth are derived. Without the operation of the revolving planetary system there would be no calendar, much less a way to measure days, much less a person's age.

God set the earth in time while man was created for the eternal. Man was not designed to die or be sick. Man was made to live in, be filled with, and exist in and out of the Glory of God. The original atmosphere of the earth was the Glory of God. The Glory of God is His total manifest presence. Man was created to live in this atmosphere, or Glory of God. Man had the distinction of possessing the DNA of God. He was God-breathed. He was God inspired. He was God's being on the earth. He was ageless, created to live in, and for, eternity even as His Creator in His realm.

Time is not one of the characteristics of the Glory of God. Time is defined by days, months, seasons, and years. But God was not, and is not, defined by time. This explains why the church has misunderstood the power of the supernatural realm of God. There is no set time to the power of God.

Miracles are in a higher realm, without the influence of time, while our circumstances are the product of time. A circumstance is an occurrence within a period of time with a beginning and an end. Imagine standing in a circle where there is a start and finish. The only thing that can break this circle of time is faith.

Faith is a higher law than time. Faith is the ascent out of time into the eternal. We are so crises orientated we do not perceive, or see, the Glory of God because we have conformed to the sense realm. What we are actually seeing complies with intellectualism and fact, not truth. Faith operates from the law of truth, not fact.

For example, your circumstances are temporal. This in itself is a fact. But in the name of Jesus, you are not operating on fact, but on the truth. The truth is, by His stripes you are healed. Truth will always supersede fact and intellectualism because God revealed truth in the person of Jesus Christ who said, "I am the way, the truth, and the life" John 14:6. Therefore, to the man who knows his rights as a citizen of Heaven, time is made to serve him. Man was not designed to serve time.

Time is a part of matter, not a matter of time. Time is not a part of faith. Faith is God's matter. It is the substance, or material, which represents elements which are made by God to serve an eternal purpose. Time was designed and created specifically for this earth. It does not exist outside this planet. The Heavens are governed by the Glory, which is the realm of eternity where there is no time, as we know it, upon this earth.

Therefore, when we are caught up into the Glory, we experience His "timelessness". It is another world. It is impossible to separate the presence of God from eternity, or timelessness.

Scientists have made a discovery which should make us think. They discovered the speed of light is slowing down. This is because eternity is invading time, and the dominant realm, eternity, displaces time as the two worlds collide.

Heaven is coming closer to earth with the advent of the glorious Day of the Lord. We are at the consummation of time, early in the morning on the third day, when Heaven's atmosphere is invading the earth. This Heavenly atmosphere brings with it the eternal realm of the Glory.

Time, as we know it on this earth, is a created thing. It is the fruit of the creation of the sun, moon and stars, all given to man so he could "measure his days". This is also known as fourth day light. These elements were created on the fourth day of creation recorded in Genesis. The light of the Glory, however, is first day light. This is the light of God Himself, emanating from His being, which came into being when He said, "*And God said, Let there be light: and there was light.*" (Genesis 1:3)

This was His light, not the created light of the sun. To understand time it is necessary to understand light. Time is a product of created light, which is defined by the scope of God's chain of events required to facilitate His purpose.

God gave the earth a time lease because of the fall of man. The fall of man changed the scope of time. Remember, time, as we know it did not exist before creation. Something had to cause time to be called forth.

Since the fall, the spiritual atmosphere within the earth is pressurized by God's increased, and enhanced, presence set forth in time though His prophecy given to man. God's timing in the earth is prophetic, much like we see in the patterns of the Jewish feasts. When we spend time studying these feasts, we will understand how God moves in cycles and patterns.

God's way to uncover these patterns and cycles is through revelation knowledge. Revelation is supernatural knowledge. And revelation comes according to the purpose, timing, and the will of God. Faith comes out of the revealed Word, which empowers us to see into the things that are unseen.

God has given us dominion over his creation. Psalms 8:6 (NKJV) says, "You have made him (man) to have dominion over the works of Your hands; You have put all things under his feet."

These are the days when great Glory is being restored, and manifested, throughout the Body of Christ. The remnant will arise to a new level of authority, and dominion, over the earth as it steps into the fullness of the measure of the stature of Christ.

As the first man was created to have this dominion, the remnant in this hour will be the fulfillment of that purpose. The remnant will also be the fulfillment of the first man. The remnant is the new man coming forth on the earth. We are about to see the full manifestation of the resurrection power of Jesus Christ as the Bride arises from childhood to maturity. Hallelujah!

God is giving us back dominion over the earth realm, and the authority to affect, and effect, what happens in, and upon, it. Therefore, relatively speaking, we have dominion over time under His authority and His power. If we have been given this privilege to take dominion over time, we can go beyond the confines of the realm of time by accessing the Glory of God. In order to access His Glory, we must learn the key to entering that realm. Presenting yourself as a vessel of worship is the key to accessing the realm of the Glory of God, and it is in this realm we obtain our miracles. We cannot obtain the miraculous by any other means. Some instruct us to wait on the Lord for the miracle, but if God intended for us to be limited to time only, He would never have given us faith.

This is the hour to believe by faith and not sight. Faith is now.

****

"God is giving us back dominion over the earth realm."

****

The unseen world is constantly disturbing the seen world because there are things being deposited in the earth from the eternal prophetic Word, that was designed and planned for the now. In actuality, that which was being seen by the prophets in a future tense, is now being seen in a present tense. What is seen in the Spirit is being disturbed by eternity invading time. Faith brings God on the scene. Things do not remain the same. God is changing things right now. The remnant is acutely aware of these changes, while the sedentary church overlooks what God is doing. As you worship, you enter the realm of the Glory of God. When your past sees your future, it realizes it cannot go where you are heading. As you step into your future; religion, unbelief and tradition become classed as negative spiritual gravity. This negative gravity keeps you conformed to the spiritual status quo. It stops you from being transformed and having your mind renewed. It will keep you in a state of being a babe, carnal or lukewarm, and leave you with a form of godliness which denies the power thereof.

The survival of religion depends on our willingness to remain ignorant of His Word. We are instructed in the Word of God to turn away from those who have arrived at this state of apostasy. Yet, many are content to sit under the leadership of a babe, carnal, or lukewarm leader. Some are thrilled to call those who deny the power of God their spiritual head.

Now we know why religion is antagonistic to Godly change. It cannot handle this kind of change. Godly change requires a relinquishing of control making one totally dependent, and reliant, on God. The systems of religion, or negative spiritual gravity, then becomes powerless. The term denomination is an unusual one. The actual term is used in the manufacturing of currency. We have denominations of one dollar bills, fives, tens, twenties, fifties, hundreds and so forth. When I think of the term denominationalism now, I think of a system by which one can count with. It is nothing more than a numerical system where the numbers are more important than the spiritual well-being of those who make up the Body.

I have even had some of my ministerial brethren say they often feel like nothing more than a number in the organization they belong to. That is so sad. But the truth is hard to take sometimes. Any system you find yourself in which does not better you in the kingdom of Heaven may be making you bitter! It may not be going where God is calling you to. Religion cannot go where God is taking you. You are on a much different course! In the last days there will be a remnant left of those who have come out from among the Laodicean church. The Bride of Christ is being prepared. Now is the accepted time for you to change into what God intended you to be before the foundations of the earth was laid. Get ready for a new thing! Follow the cloud of the Glory of God.

I was ministering in a church in Tulsa, Oklahoma in 1999. It was as if I had left the earth and entered Heaven. I saw the earth spinning with the Heavens traveling toward the earth. Then the Heavens literally stood still in divine alignment over the earth. A door to the Throne Room opened and the River of God gushed forth like a gigantic, global Niagara Falls.

I heard the Lord speak and say, *"The current is changing. Look at the Heavens and hear My voice. The way it is changing is that no person will be a reference point. It will only be Me. Ask my servants how they can claim to be coming before Me and deny the River. Watch! The waves are changing."*

From my vantage point a giant wave came on Tulsa and I saw Richard Roberts on his face crying out to God for revival. His tears became part of the River. The Lord continued, "I am going to visit Tulsa and manifest signs like they have never seen before." Then I saw Richard standing with his father, Oral, next to him. Oral stepped into Richard and the two became one

The Lord said, *"I am consummating the waves. I am consummating the mantles that this father had into a new thing. It will not be the same but a different stream. It is not so much a change of the guard, but it is much more like the changing of the waves. As one flows out, the other flows in. In this case there will be a difference in the size and power of the waves. There will be waves there that have never been on earth before."*

The waves lingered over Oral Roberts University. They started to flow to places in Tulsa and stay in places that are virtually unknown to the inhabitants of the city. The vision lasted about twenty minutes. God replayed the entire vision as I entered the sanctuary and began to minister. The prophetic word came forth for nearly thirty minutes.

The Lord continued, *"Say this as a watchword! Tell them, the current is changing. It is not what you think. You cannot go into a service expecting the same old thing. You have to learn to minister out of this new current."*

The River of God went around certain parts of Tulsa. I asked the Lord, *"How come the river is not going over all of Tulsa?"*

The Lord responde*d, "Some of them are in deception." I asked the Lord to explain what He was saying to me. This is what He replied, "The deception is this: This is what they will say, which will cause them to miss the new wave of My Glory, 'We have seen it all before.' There are waves approaching the earth that have never been seen before. Do you think that all of those former waves were all there was? The end time church is nearer My return than they could ever imagine. The nearer to the Throne they get, they will not be able to speak. All they will be able to say is, 'It is God.' Now you know why there are some things that I will reveal on the spur of the moment. There will be people who will begin to take the credit for this new wave of My Glory. When they do, the current will bypass them, for I am unstoppable."*

A dean from Oral Roberts University sitting in the meeting took the tape of the prophecy and said, "Richard has been crying out to God for days." A new wave hit Oral Roberts University and revival continued for a season. God was true to His Word.

We are living in an exciting time in the history of the world, and the Body of Christ. There is nothing taking place, concerning the Body, that is void of spiritual significance. Everything is happening according to God's plan and timetable. But as great as the church is, and has been in the past, there is so much that is yet to be done to prepare the Bride for the Bridegroom. Statistics report that about two-thirds of the world's population, four billion souls, are outside of the Kingdom of God.

Are we assuming that the Body of Christ is actually three billion souls strong? To be honest, this does not reflect what the Bible classifies as the remnant. We are told that in the last days there will be a great falling away. Where else would this take place if it were not inside the walls of the church?

The world cannot fall from a height it has not reached. Wake up church! There are those among us who are not of Him. But more tragically than that is that there are those among us today that are of Him today that will not be of Him tomorrow. And there will be a great falling away before Jesus comes for

His bride. Wake up church! The hour is at hand. As Jesus said to His disciples in Matthew 24:4 (KJV) "*Take heed that no man deceive you.*"

The church continues to be plagued with multiple kinds of diseases, infirmities and sins. Family relationships are being destroyed with divorce rates which have exceeded the ratio in the world. A well-known research group on the west coast reports that for every three persons entering the ministry, five are leaving the ministry. Those who once had a powerful anointing are trading their position in the fivefold to become life coaches. Why is this happening? It is because the power of God is not evident in their life. They are seeking their own ends, for their own gain. When the church fails to satisfy their fleshly desires, they will turn to worldly ways. What an opportunity and challenge for healing, deliverance and restoration. Now is the opportune time for the Body of Christ to press in and pursue the greater things of God that are breaking out in the earth.

I Corinthians 2:9-10 states; "*But as it is written, Eye hath not seen, nor ear heard, neither have entered into the heart of man, the things which God hath prepared for them that love Him. But God hath revealed them unto us by his Spirit.*"

We are going to witness, in these last days, demonstrations of His love and power through miracles, signs and wonders. These manifestations will leave us speechless and in awe of Him. This is not a time for business as usual. In fact, God is demanding that we operate by His principle. Neither can we operate from those models of operation which used to work in the past. God is doing a new thing. And for the Body to align itself with this new thing will require letting go of the old.

> *"No man putteth a piece of new cloth unto an old garment, for that which is put in to fill it up taketh from the garment, and the rent is made worse. Neither do men put new wine into old bottles: else the bottles break, and the wine runneth out, and the bottles perish: but they put new wine into new bottles, and both are preserved."* (Matthew 9:16-17)

The truth which lies herein is profound, and yet it is plain. The old cannot be mixed with the new. The old cannot contain the new. In the early church this Scripture applied to the mixing of Judaism and Christianity. They could not mix together because of the limited capacity in each one for the other. In these last days we will see that it is impossible for the old school of thought to mix with the new mindset of the remnant. The new mindset is being brought forth in and by the revelation, and manifestation, of the Glory of God today by the Holy Spirit with the invasion of eternity invading time.

As we have already stated, Godly change is hard for the church to embrace. If they cannot tolerate Godly change, then they will certainly not embrace the new which He is bringing about. The church is now entering into and living in a season of expectancy for the fullness of the Word "exceeding abundantly beyond all that we can ask or think, " as stated in Ephesians 3:20. There is nothing in the unseen world that is going to remain unseen. We don't have much time left. The lease God has granted to the earth is about to be cancelled.

These events, which are even at the door, will not happen by conventional means or by the household names of people we know. This new wave, this new move of God will not be heard of in the media. Neither will this move of God have a reference point as did the faith movement. What He will do on earth before Jesus returns will not need a human reference point. The only reference will be the Holy Spirit revealing Jesus to all mankind in the fullness of His Glory through the saints, His Body, each a living stone of His Temple. Hallelujah!

The gospel without signs and wonders is invalid. The gospel says that signs will follow the Word.

"And they went forth, and preached every where, the Lord working with them, and confirming the word with signs following."(Mark 16:20)

However, if the Word of God is preached, then there will be signs following. In our meetings today we are regularly seeing manifestations of the presence of God as He releases His Glory. The Word is penetrating the hearts, transforming the very being and existence of those hearing with joy and expectancy. His unsolicited signs, wonders and miracles flow into our meetings without prompting. Oh, Glory to God, what an honor it is to have His presence in these meetings. We are so grateful to Him for showing Himself to us in so many exciting ways. All we can do is shout, "Thank You, Lord!"

Renny McLean

CHAPTER THREE

The Realm of
Prophetic Vision

"Man seems to have the unique ability to see beyond the present, into the future. He is most adept at this when he invents and creates those entities which change the course of society."
- Unknown

When God speaks to His Apostles, Prophets, Evangelists, Pastors and Teachers, He often will cause them to dream or have visions. All throughout the Word of God there are instances of visions occurring which set the destiny of nations in place. I have met many people around the world who have come to me and told me they had a vision or a dream. Many wanted me to interpret the vision or dream for them. In some cases, I was given a Rhema Word for them, while other times I was as mystified as they were as to the meaning.

Throughout my life I have had many open visions. An open vision is where you are fully awake and can see not only the environment around you, but also have the ability to look into the supernatural realm. One of the more interesting aspects to these open visions is the attention given to detail. There is nothing hazy about what is shown me. In fact, all too often the reasons for what I am seeing are being explained to me as I witness them. While I have been ministering in the pulpit, I have had many visions which were so overpowering, I had to relate them to the congregation, while other times I was directed to keep them to myself until otherwise instructed.

Over the years God has been so kind to have shared with me on this level several times. Some visions warned me of impending circumstances I was to be watchful of, while others were tools to sharpen my understanding of His realm, and what was awaiting us on that glorious day when He says time is no more and He calls us into His presence. Early visions would show me those particular nations I was to go to. Some would show me the faces of those who I did not know but would come to know. In each and every circumstance, I was constantly reminded I was viewing another dimension, one where man and woman had originally come from. It was that atmosphere where He dwelt and desired us to dwell in with Him.

What more wonders there are to behold, I do not know. I am assured I have not seen it all.

As His Word states in 1 Corinthians 2:9, *"Eye hath not seen, nor ear heard, neither have entered into the heart of man, the things which God hath prepared for them that love him."*

There is no better way, other than by seeing and experiencing, to find out what "God is doing" than by sharing testimonials of those things He is doing. Therefore, I want to share some of the testimonials of the varied manifestations and phenomenon which we have witnessed in our meetings.

However, before I share them, allow me to speak from my heart with you for a moment. So many people have asked me about some of the unusual phenomenon that are written about within the testimonials that are to follow. To be completely honest with you, I do not have an answer for those who are seeking some kind of traditional response.

Much of what I am seeing in our ministry these days is as new to me as it is to you, and to those it is happening to. Over the years I have come to accept these things which are clearly unexplainable marvels as signs, wonders and miracles. One of the basic fundamental premises of our ministry is that we must honor the doctrine of Jesus Christ which is given to us in the form of six principles found in Hebrews 6:1-2:

> *"Therefore leaving the principles of the doctrine of Christ, let us go on unto perfection; not laying again the foundation of repentance from dead works, and of faith toward God, of the doctrine of baptisms, and of laying on of hands, and of resurrection of the dead, and of eternal judgment."*

Essentially these principles of Christ are very specifically identified as the responsibilities of the babes in Christ. One does not go on to perfection until these principles are fulfilled by those babes; one of those principles is the doctrine of the laying on of hands, which is not evident in the majority of the cultural churches today, as an example. How do we expect to enter into and understand those new things which will appear as we mature into the fullness of Christ until we have come into fullness of understanding the basics? In Hebrews 5:12 the "baby" saints are being disciplined with these words:

"For when for the time ye ought to be teachers, ye have need that one teach you again which be the first principles of the oracles of God." (Hebrews 5:12)

Then, Hebrews 6:3 gives us a clear statement, in the context of Hebrews 5 and 6 that God is not going to permit us to go on to maturity until the basics are finished.

The following testimonies reflect what took place while I was teaching the Word in some of our meetings. As the Glory of God fell on the place we were meeting in, the faith of those present made a demand on Him to heal them. I had nothing to do with these miracles happening. I just witnessed them and give God the Glory.

I have seen the dead raised, as well as having witnessed many creative miracles, which restored damaged and missing body parts, as well as the healing of many different diseases and infirmities. We have seen God heal sexually transmitted diseases, even AIDS, not to mention financial miracles.

We have seen God heal relationships which appeared to be headed for the divorce court. We have rejoiced with those who have found their way back to the path the Lord had prepared for them and have watched the hand of God set free those who were in bondage and imprisoned with bitterness. But, I am convinced that we have not seen anything yet compared to what our God is about to do in this end time season. We have begun to see the results of His resurrection power in a greater and mightier way.

So, as you read these testimonies allow the Holy Spirit to quicken your Spirit man in order for you to know the revelation of God is being manifested in the earthly realm.

In Ohio, a lady who came to our meeting was experiencing supernatural oil and the presence of the Lord fell all over. For two days she was aware of the Lord dealing with her mouth and was confessing that the Lord would purify her speech. The next day, during a service the Glory of God fell and released a miracle while I was speaking, and she received eight gold teeth in her mouth. She is a sign and wonder.

As the Glory of God fell in another meeting, a missionary lady received a supernatural multiplication of money. She gave what she had and then was grieved she did not have more to give. When she reached in her pocket there was the exact amount that she had just given. She promptly gave that in the offering. Some moments later someone gave her back the same amount. God gave her back what she gave in the beginning.

In Houston, Texas, the Glory fell during the meeting with such magnitude that hundreds of people received miracles. Tumors vanished and legs and arms were healed. One brother who was involved in a court case asked for a financial miracle. Within days he received a check for $1,500,000. Yet this miracle is no greater than any of the others.

In an Ohio meeting, a lady kept disturbing the service by calling out, "I want to testify!" "Well, praise the Lord," I responded. She then replied, "But something else has happened." She insisted I give her the microphone and she proceeded to say, "I was here the other night when the Glory of God fell. As the presence of the Lord fell, God began dealing with me and my finances. I knew I had received a miracle." The following day she had a phone call confirming a government contract for $53 million. Several weeks later we went back to the same church. The pastor said, "The sister that received the contract is in France. She wants you to call her." When I called her she told me, "I have something incredible to tell you. When I got to France, they canceled the $53 million dollar contract, and changed it to an $83 million dollar contract!"

In a meeting in Atlanta, Georgia, two crippled people were in the audience. During the service the Lord said to me, "Tell the people to stand up and start walking." I told the whole church to stand up and start walking. As the whole church obeyed, including the lame, all of a sudden, the Glory of the Lord fell in a mighty way. I remember this one woman, who had been crippled with multiple sclerosis. As she walked, she broke into a dance.

I recall seeing a lady I have known for many years in one of our Glory Summits. Her arm was broken in several places. There was no mention of healing, then all of a sudden, her hand straightened out and she began to move it. She knew she had been healed. She made her way to the platform, and with great excitement informed us she had experienced a miracle. When she returned to her home, she went to the doctor to have her arm examined. The physician was astounded and did not believe her. "I have never seen this before," he stated to her. "I don't know how to tell you this, but your bones are actually fresh— brand new." She knew what had happened. Now her doctor did, too. All it took was for her to worship and the miracle manifested. To God be the Glory!

In a meeting in Texas, I recall a three-day meeting where the Glory of the Lord was manifesting as people were worshipping. On one particular evening there, a lady came wearing a brace on her leg. I told her, "Just take it off," not really aware of the magnitude of what had just transpired. In obedience to the spoken word, she removed the brace, to find she could walk with ease all around the building. This triggered another miracle. Another woman, who was bound to a wheelchair, was gloriously healed. She stood up from the wheelchair and began to follow the other lady around the building. Miracles started raining down upon the meeting!

Several weeks after that meeting, a testimony came to us from the sister with the leg brace. When she went to the hospital the doctors were bewildered. She was scheduled to have a steel pin surgically implanted into her leg that week. When the technicians looked at the x-ray, they saw newly formed bone in her leg.

I was asked to preach in a meeting in Philadelphia, where a great hunger for the presence, and power, of God was prevalent. It was overwhelming to see so many lifting their hands in total surrender to God's Glory, as they were brought into His presence through their worship. Time was suspended. It had no meaning. It had lost its grip on the people. As we entered His manifested presence, there was a sense in the atmosphere that this was the moment for anything to happen. We had taken the limitations off God. The word impossible never crossed our minds. It was as if we had eliminated it from our vocabulary. We were locked into that moment in time for God's power to manifest.

As I was preaching, I began declaring what I was seeing. I started to declare deaf ears to open, cancers and tumors to dissolve and dissipate in Jesus' name. Suddenly, the platform was filled with miraculous testimonies. The number of those healed from deafness was more than fifty. They now stood on the platform, hearing by the word, and power, of God. It was thrilling to see so many deaf healed. But after having them examined, over half of them informed us that they had no eardrums at all before their miracle. What incredible creative miracles took place that night. God had created eardrums on a grand scale! Additionally, there were at least thirty people with tumors suddenly disappearing. Several tumors, some the size of a man's fist, were now obliterated by the power of God.

****

"I have received a miracle!"

****

As I was walking off the platform, a lady ran up to me, grabbed hold of my coat and said, "Brother Renny, I have received a miracle!" To which I replied, "Praise God!" I asked her what the Lord had done for her. She was one of the women who experienced a tumor supernaturally vanishing. She said the Lord had done something else. "What has the Lord done for you", I asked. "Look in my mouth," she said. Up to this point in our ministry, we had witnessed gold teeth and gold fillings in abundance, so I was expecting to see a tooth filled with gold; however, there was no gold. The woman got more than excited and kept insisting that I look in her mouth. When I took a look, everything looked quite normal. She implored me to look again into her mouth. This was a bit amusing to me as I didn't see anything out of the ordinary. Finally, she looked at me and smiled. "Brother Renny, you just don't get it," she said. "No, I don't get it," I responded. "When I came into the service tonight, I didn't have one tooth in my mouth!" This forty-eight-year-old woman had a full set of brand-new teeth. To this day she cannot stop talking about what God had done for her. And we hear she smiles all the time. You would too, wouldn't you?

The following night her dentist came to the meeting to see for himself. He went to the platform, with the woman's dental records in hand, and confirmed that God had produced a miracle. What an extraordinary start to a meeting, and this was only the second night!

An entire series of creative miracles were unfolding. The following night we witnessed the lame walking. Eighteen believers threw their crutches and canes away. Some got up from their wheelchairs as the Glory moved through the building.

During this meeting, the Lord gave me a Rhema word, which was as follows: *"If you bring the high praise unto Me, there will be a continual opening in the Heavens, spiraling upward, as you touch higher realms where even greater miracles are awaiting to manifest on the earth."*

I think it wise to stop here and emphatically state that we, in and of ourselves, cannot manufacture or manipulate miracles. They are acts of a sovereign God. We are simply the witnesses of His Glory.

I have seen God perform creative miracles for the last twenty years in my ministry. I know the key to the operation of this realm is the ability to access the faith realm and break the constraints of the time realm. Some years ago, Ruth Heflin asked me to take her place at a Catholic retreat where there were 900 highly esteemed Catholic priests. They gave me forty-five minutes to speak. How do you minister to all the needs and allow God to move in power in less than an hour?

Fortunately, they were hungry for the supernatural, and God showed up in a powerful way. During that meeting the Glory fell and over fifty deaf ears were opened. More than half of them had been born without eardrums, yet God created eardrums for them in that meeting.

Why are we surprised and limited in our thinking concerning creative miracles? We think it not strange that God can cause our hair to grow, our nails to grow and our cells to replenish themselves. Yet we have trouble believing God can create a missing or damaged body part. Let go of such limited thinking. It is well within the scope of God's ability to grow new teeth, eyeballs, bones, and eardrums. Looking at the creative ability of God in the negative separates us from the supernatural, from our miracle, be it a financial miracle, a healing miracle, or a miracle in relationships. Whatever the need, we must change our perception of time to unlock the supernatural. Whatever reason we give God for why He cannot do things for us is the reason He won't do it for us.

In that same meeting we saw twenty-five cancers disappear. At that meeting twelve wheelchairs were miraculously emptied. Only when we stand before the Lord will we truly know all that happened in those services. So often, God does things in His secret place.

****

"There is no distance, or time, when it comes to prayer."

****

Many in the medical field will acknowledge that God heals, but then they'll attempt to minimize the miracle by saying, "They would have recovered anyway, given time." When God interferes with the natural order of time and speeds things up, it is called a miracle.

I was ministering in a church in Houston, Texas. The pastor had invited me, and other ministers present at the services, to come to his home for some refreshment. While at his home, he received a call from the hospital that his grandson was seriously ill. Then in a few moments another call came announcing that the grandson had passed away. Emotions were understandably high, as this was the first grandson. I told the pastor, "There is no distance, or time, when it comes to prayer. God can give us a creative miracle even without us being there." Sensing the urgency of the situation, I began to inquire of the Lord concerning what He would have me do. Suddenly, a Rhema word exploded in my spirit. I asked the group to join hands and pray. I began to declare that life return to this young man's body.

After a season of prayer, the phone rang once more with news that the young man had suddenly, and miraculously, begun to breathe again on his own. Here was a young man who had been dead but was now alive! To God be the Glory.

The dictionary defines the word "creative" as follows: Having the ability or power to create things. Creating; productive. Characterized by originality and expressiveness; imaginative.

To give you an example of what I am talking about, let me share with you one of the most wonderful creative miracles I was ever able to witness. In Maine, there was a family with twin sons. One of the sons had perfect eyes, while the other had no color in the pupil area. During the service the Glory of God was so powerful it caused the father's faith to rise to such a level that he left the auditorium and went to the nursery where the twin boys were being cared for. He lifted up the son with no color in his pupils and brought him into the service. I was not aware that any of this was going on. We were singing and worshipping as the Spirit of God was so wonderfully present. As the service progressed, we began to take testimonies. The father walked up to the platform, holding his son in his arms, and shared with us a most unusual testimony. While we were worshipping, he looked down at his son and was shocked to see that his son's white eye pupils were filled with the most beautiful color of blue. What a glorious miracle for this child, family, and church.

One of our partners, Pauline, followed us up and down the country. She said, "As soon as I heard you were going to be at Pastor Tony Miller's church, the Lord said for me to bring this man to you. He had a fight with his father and needs prayer" I replied, "Okay, bring him and I will pray for him." After the service, she brought this young man to me. What I was to learn in those next few moments was that this young man did not have any eyes.

When I prayed for him, the Lord said, "Put your hands on his eyes." I was still looking at the empty sockets when I was to hear God call them eyeballs! As I laid my hands on the young man, I saw Heaven open in a flash. When that happened, my hand jerked, and in my hand I saw an eyeball. The Lord said, "It's there; now declare it." I felt it come into my hand and go out of my hand into the empty sockets. When I removed my hands, he had two healthy, normal eyeballs.

I have been walking in miracles since I was ten years of age. I saw the dead raised when I was fourteen. I saw eyes appear where there were none. I saw ears materialize where there were none. I saw missing body parts supernaturally develop since I was ten, and there is no way to document everything I have seen in my ministry. Have you ever attended a meeting where there is a great crowd, but of the hundreds that come up, one only sticks out in your mind? That is the one you were apt to document. But when you thought about it, you realized how many more there were. At just twenty years of age, I was at a church in England where a brother was in a wheelchair sitting before me. About seven wheelchairs were emptied that night. I said to the brother, "Rise and be healed." There were crutches everywhere that night. The Lord said, "Don't touch him. Just tell him, 'Rise and be healed.'" He looked at me as if I was a little crazy. I understand that. Half the church thinks that. Eventually he got up and moved, and then he started to walk perfectly. When I left that church, the news had been in the papers for six weeks. Someone sent me the clipping. The headlines read: "Man born with no ankle bones received ankle bones." Your job is not to try to understand the miracle. Your job is to let the miracle work itself. You will never have a problem if you just let God do it.

****

"Just declare it healed."

****

I was at a three-night meeting in a Boston church, and lady with a leg brace was there the first night. I knew nothing about her situation. During worship I saw a leg brace in my spirit. The Lord said, "Just declare it healed." As I spoke the words, it was obvious people didn't believe it. Nothing ever happens up there, so why should they believe now? I said, "There is a leg condition being healed in the back of the room." In my spirit I saw the leg brace and God said, "I will give her a sign so she will know it is Me." The sign was this: As soon as I declared the word, the leg brace unfastened itself and fell to her feet. She picked up the leg brace and started waving it. What a mighty God of signs, wonders and miracles we serve! Another woman had a serious eye infection. Her eye was diseased and colorless, and the doctors were preparing to remove it. The Spirit told me, "Just slap her eye quickly and hold it. Don't remove your hand...Now remove it." When I removed my hand, she had a clear, healthy eye with normal color and appearance. A farsighted Filipino sister was sitting in the front row. I told her, "Cover your good eye. Follow my finger." God restored her vision instantly.

In a meeting in Tulsa, I was caught up in the Spirit for several hours. That one night turned to four weeks. No one was in their seat. We were oblivious to time. The living creatures came into the meeting. A lady in the crowd had cancer of the liver and it had metastasized to the brain. I don't like to pray for people's healing because Jesus did not pray for the sick. His Word was sufficient. I am anointed, speak the Word. My Lord is my example. I do pray for the people but now I believe more in using my faith to bring people into the presence of God letting the Glory of God do the rest. In the early days of revival it was, "Just believe." Now I believe it is, "Just enter in." That bypasses your struggle, and the Glory of God does the rest.

One woman in particular was caught up in the Spirit for three hours. She froze, unable to move. She was on dialysis for a ravaged liver. While in the spirit, she physically felt the hand of God move inside of her body. She knew it was a miracle. When the doctor examined her, he said, "You have a new liver. It doesn't even correspond to the one you had before." Pay attention, Church; just get into the presence of God and let Him do the rest.

At a meeting in England, there was a boy who had no bones in his arms. While praying for the sick that night, I clearly saw bones. I did not know exactly what bones I was seeing, but all of sudden, I said, "Father, I declare bones into someone's arm right now." When we took testimonies after the meeting, there was a ten-year-old boy who was born without arm bones. The following day, he went to his doctor who discovered that bones had grown where originally there were none. We must mature to the stage where we declare what we see. There are some things in the realm of the Spirit for which man declares the timeframe, not God. Faith is now. Declare means to bring something forward. You don't have to wait for it to happen. You can bring it forth and it will manifest now. In the realm of the Spirit, prophecy, as we know, it is going to change. In prophecy, we look to revival, but we don't take it now. If it's a healing, it may take weeks, but a miracle is here and now. In the realm of the Spirit, we declare what we see in the Spirit realm.

When you declare something, it is framed. It's a done deal. You weren't educated to it, and because you weren't, you couldn't cooperate with it. Accordingly, if you can be uneducated about your disease, your debt, your lack, etc., it can't cooperate with you. Do you have ears to hear what the Spirit is saying? How many of you are cooperating with cancer? Are you cooperating with your debt? Anything you cooperate with speeds up your circumstance. Satan just hates this kind of revelation because when you "know that you know" you're there, you'll have no choice but to become the realm you are walking in. Walk in the Glory!

Renny McLean

CHAPTER FOUR

Perceiving the
Realm of the Miraculous

"For the scientist who has lived by his faith in the power of reason, the story ends like a bad dream. He has scaled the mountains of ignorance; he is about to conquer the highest peak; as he pulls himself over the final rock, he is greeted by a band of theologians who have been sitting there for centuries."
-Robert Jastrow, a self-proclaimed agnostic

Daniel 12:4 says, *"But thou, O Daniel, shut up the words, and seal the book, even to the time of the end: many shall run to and fro, and knowledge shall be increased."*

I believe these times are much like what the Bible spoke of when the seals are broken, and man's knowledge of good and evil increases. People are running to and fro in search of knowledge. The buzz word is information. Information has become so important that we are carrying around handheld computers which will allow us instant access to the vast resources of data around the world. We now can take instant pictures of events and send them to our friends and loved ones with the click of a button. A man can stand on one continent and send a text message, or make a long-distance call, simply by using a cellular phone. Many luxury cars are equipped with a tracking device making it possible to know exactly where the car is in case of theft or requiring repair.

Put this seed thought in your Spirit man. Common sense is to the natural man what revelation is to the man in the Glory of God.

When God does something new, it contradicts religious doctrine. Many religious leaders stand on historical data rather than revelation data. Now, that does not mean that all historical study is invalid. Quite the opposite. There is a trend among many Christians who have come out of ecclesiastical settings to want to discard those lessons learned from the early years of Christianity. Luther's reformation was one of the most powerful turning points in the history of religion. His edict "The Just Shall Live By Faith" was one that set free thousands of those searching for the grace and mercy of God.

Coming from England, I am aware that there are differences in how we communicate. To give you an example, here in America when someone says to a cabbie, "Take me downtown fast," the general answer would be, "No problem." In England, if you told the cabbie those same words, he might respond by saying, "Okay mate, hop in we'll be there in a jiffy." It's just the way they say it. After all these years in the United States I have come to realize that the church has adopted certain catch phrases. It all too often makes an outsider feel a bit uncomfortable when they first enter our services, because they are not accustomed to our dialogue. The phrase "keep it real" should apply to us in these last days. We must communicate the Kingdom of God in the terminology of Heaven, not religion.

Christians often quote a Scripture that is not found in the Bible, but we say it so many times that it sticks in our minds, and we believe it as coming from the Bible. Cleanliness is next to Godliness is not in the Word. It is a great statement, but just not Scriptural. In these last days we are hearing a great many voices proclaiming the Word of the Lord. Many are declaring doctrine, while others are declaring revelation. If you are spiritually discerning, you will be able to tell the difference between revelation and doctrine.

The Church is a mystery, a revelation! We cannot define it by some philosophical approach, much less a denominational approach. There is coming a day when all arguments will cease. He will make His Word come to pass. He will reveal the fullness of His Glory. It's sad to say, but many will be in the halls of higher learning roaring out their rhetoric so furiously they will not hear Him call to them. And then they will be left to live out what they debated, to see if they were right or wrong. And the debate will be a heated one, you can count on that. Beloved, His Word does not lie. What He has revealed in His Word will come to pass exactly as He said it would.

In these end times the Glory of the Lord is being revealed. For instance, when a door of utterance is open, God gives us a vocabulary we've never had before. We are infused with a supernatural intelligence we did not possess prior to the utterance. Often, an utterance will bring clarity to a situation concerning the kingdom of Heaven. Other times, it will address the local assembly of believers. He will always speak to edify, lift up and encourage His children.

Truth is called upon according to the hunger of the people. You cannot preach what you prepared when you are sensitive to hear what the Spirit is saying to the church. As soon as you stand, that revelatory realm comes, and you must begin to speak what you hear in the Glory. Let me speak to those who are in the leadership of the church for a moment. We must cease from becoming "professional pulpit orators". It is a well-known fact that thousands of pastors are downloading their messages from a service which offers a manuscript for them to read each Sunday. In fact, the service even offers them a visual aid to place on the overhead screen. Why seek a Word from God when you can get it from the Internet? Then, when the church begins to dwindle in size, the pastors wonder what is wrong! The people are hungry for fresh manna, not some day-old bread.

During a meeting the Lord spoke to me by an open vision of a scroll. On the scroll were these words: *"In the latter days it will come to pass that my people will speak by open vision. There will be a memory loss as to what they know. When the cloud is present, they will speak things that are conducive to those things I will show them in the cloud."*

What He meant by the phrase "there will be a memory loss as to what they know" simply means His people will give up, throw away and discard the old paradigms which they held to for so long.

They will begin to see into the invisible realm of the supernatural. They will speak differently because their relationship has changed! The more intimate we are with Him, our language changes.

All about Heaven is not written. I have been to Heaven on several occasions and believe me there is no way I can tell you all I heard and saw. How could one write about all that was seen in Heaven? If you can't write everything you see on earth, what makes you think you can write all you see in the Heavenlies? There are still many mysteries to be revealed. Heaven is the only place in eternity that is named, and yet, Heaven is created. Heaven is the Capitol of Eternity. That is why it is a city.

We are coming to that place where God is going to manifest this among the people. Stop putting things in the future when God says it is now.

"And immediately I was in the spirit: and, behold, a throne was set in heaven, and one sat on the throne. And he that sat was to look upon like a jasper and a sardine stone: and there was a rainbow round about the throne, in sight like unto an emerald. And round about the throne were four and twenty seats: and upon the seats I saw four and twenty elders sitting, clothed in white raiment; and they had on their heads crowns of gold. And out of the throne proceeded lightnings and thunderings and voices: and there were seven lamps of fire burning before the throne, which are the seven Spirits of God. And before the throne there was a sea of glass like unto crystal: and in the midst of the throne, and round about the throne, were four beasts full of eyes before and behind. And the first beast was like a lion, and the second beast like a calf, and the third beast had a face as a man, and the fourth beast was like a flying eagle. And the four beasts had each of them six wings about him; and they were full of eyes within: and they rest not day and night, saying, Holy, holy, holy, Lord God Almighty, which was, and is, and is to come. And when those beasts give glory and honour and thanks to him that sat on the throne, who liveth for ever and ever, The four and twenty elders fall down before him that sat on the throne, and worship him that liveth for ever and ever, and cast their crowns before the throne, saying, Thou art worthy, O Lord, to receive glory and honour and power: for thou hast created all things, and for thy pleasure they are and were created." (Revelation 4:2-11)

The four beasts have eyes before and behind them. In Ezekiel it says they don't go backward, they go forward. In the realm of the Spirit, the past, the present and the future is the now. They have eyes before and behind. Notice it says they have eyes within. The eye represents inner vision. Prophetically speaking, you are in a vision. It is as much real as your open vision. Everyone has a prophetic sense. One day, during a massage, a masseuse informed me that he didn't have to touch my eye with his hand to actually touch my eye. He said that the nerve to my eye is in my hand. Prophetically speaking, there are times we don't perceive anything about someone unless we touch them. So, the laying on of the hands was not the principle of impartation—it was the principle of seeing. A blind person is sightless, but can they really be blind when they can touch?

Do you know another place that corresponds to the nerve of the eye is in your feet? One of the most powerful stories written in the Bible was about Enoch. It says Enoch walked with God, which means while Enoch was walking, he was seeing. (He got caught up in the Spirit and was not.) In the Old Testament you'll often see this expression: "Lift your hands and praise the Lord." This simply means the lifting of hands was seeing in His presence. There is something powerful in meetings when the corporate body stands and lifts up their hands. It is an awesome sight. In one moment in time, we are all caught up and we all perceive. Everyone can be caught up and perceive. You don't have to be prophetic. You can be a believer and declare. You have the prophecy living within you. That apostle is living in you. He's as big in you as he is in me. Simply believe what you perceive and declare it, and God will frame it. Amen.

This seeing realm is very real. Now, envision the elders and the living creatures encircling the throne, and note that they are saying, "Holy." They have eyes in front and eyes at the back, but they are still going forward. What are they saying? Only one word, "Holy, Holy, Holy." In other words, they are not just saying the word Holy, they are actually saying what they are seeing as they go round the throne.

Here is where you must use one of those elements I spoke about in the beginning of this book. Now, you must use your vision to see this picture. If you can grasp this revelation, a new door will open to you as to how you give unto the Lord. Put this in your Spirit. The Reaper is harvesting as fast as he can. On his heels comes the Plowman. He is already preparing another harvest in the soil that the reaper has just harvested. When the two of them meet in the field there is rejoicing. Instant seeding is reaping instant harvesting! You may say to yourself that is not so. Well, what about the following passage.

"Say not ye, There are yet four months, and then cometh harvest? behold, I say unto you, Lift up your eyes, and look on the fields; for they are white already to harvest. And he that reapeth receiveth wages, and gathereth fruit unto life eternal: that both he that soweth and he that reapeth may rejoice together. And herein is that saying true, One soweth, and another reapeth. I sent you to reap that whereon ye bestowed no labour: other men laboured, and ye are entered into their labours." (John 4:35-38)

The fields are all ready. Notice the emphasis on the word. All the fields are ready to harvest. The key is to lift up your eyes, indicating a higher realm of vision, and look from that position down to the fields. The reason He spoke in this manner was to imply that we are seated with Him in Heavenly places and can take a different view of the harvest fields.

The second wonder in this passage is the unity of the laborers. They both allow the other to enter into the field and harvest, even though the other has not labored there. Here lies another wonderful image as to entering into the labor of others. That unity allowed you to partake of the fields you had never been in. Both are laboring in the field together. There is no separation on their seasons. They are no longer in the gestation of time, they are in the now. The seeding and the harvesting is no longer in relayed time. It happens suddenly and simultaneously. Can you not see this miracle? The more you plant, the more you harvest. The faster you seed, the faster you drive the reaper. Can you not see the miracle of this law of multiplication? Even before the reaper has touched the harvest, the sower has once again planted seed in the ground. There is no end to the seeding and reaping. And in both cases, neither one is actually working. The Lord of the Harvest is at work. Their labor has become worship, not sweat and toil. There is no longer a curse to their sweat equity, but an instant dividend of profit.

We must remind ourselves of the mustard seed. As tiny as it is, it has the power to move mountains.

"While the earth remaineth, seedtime and harvest, and cold and heat, and summer and winter, and day and night shall not cease." (Genesis 8:22)

There is no end to the process! We are living in the days when time in the Spirit is being greatly compressed. Creative miracles and the raising of the dead are becoming the normal mode of Apostolic ministries.

Prophetic prayer is coming to pass even as it is being prayed. What is spoken in intercession meetings is happening in the sanctuary. The Lord created His house as a house of prayer. The prayer rooms must not be exclusive areas in the house of the Lord, or some remote room hidden away from the entire Body of Christ to seek out. The entire building must be the place where prayer sets up habitation. And when we move our mentality from a place of prayer to a house of prayer, we will see the creative hand of God. Hallelujah!

Yes, it is already happening. We are seeing creative miracles restoring damaged and missing body parts. Reports are increasing of the dead being raised all over the world. There are things happening in the realm of the Spirit to which God does not give a tense. We are the ones to declare the tense. Past, present, future must be declared by us. Prophesy now, instead of later. After the fact is not prophecy. It is an exercise in prognosis.

The Lord said, *"There are realms of My Glory that have not been revealed. Everywhere you go, get My people into worship. When they worship, the door of Heaven opens, and they will see another side of My Glory and power. I have created realms in the Heavens that have not yet been revealed. The angels have not seen all the Glory in, and of, Me. The living creatures, the cherubim and seraphim have not seen all the Glory in, and of, Me. The angelic hosts have to go from Glory to Glory, you must go from Glory to Glory too."*

Whenever you are in a meeting, you should not care how long it takes, worship until the Glory life manifests. When that Glory comes, you can speak, and miracles will happen. Change your praise. There are multiple manifestations of praise. Each level represents a gear and another level. Have some diversity.

While worshipping in a meeting a pastor said, "Brother Renny, would you help me? Is there anything you would encourage us to change in our services in order to keep the Glory continuing in our church?" I said, "Singing off the lyrics projected on the wall is different from singing what is in your spirit. Your new song can take you to levels that no other can take you. Sing the new song and dance before the Lord. Until you do, you will never reach a greater level of true liberty in the spirit. Until you sing the song in you, all you will do is sing someone else's song." Each house must have its own sound. The very fact that there are different mixes of musicians, singers and composers in each congregation gives room for a distinctive sound to come forth.

All too often, we prefer to sing what is on the top ten hit worship list instead of singing what the spirit is saying to the hearts of the members of our congregations. I would be willing to say that there are poets, songwriters and writers of all description in your church. The key is to allow their expressions to be manifested. Of course, there will be a season in the beginning where the fluidity might not be as we want it, but given time it will create a new sound in the house.

If you are wanting to reach the nations you must have the sound of the nations in the house. That does not mean that you have to have a certain groove sound to attract the different cultures. What it does mean is that you have the sound of worship which calls to those individuals who are seeking that certain sound in the Glory.

When there is liberty no one has to tell you what to do, or when to do it. You just feel free to act as the Spirit leads. God wants you to feel free to run, to dance, to bless the Lord with all your actions.

Put this as a wisdom seed in your spirit. Have you noticed that the Glory is the strongest when the song is live? When recorded music is used, the voice is live but the music isn't, so it does not build the greater atmosphere. If the music is live, then there is a praise inside of you that will bring the Glory cloud realm. When God's people hold back their praises, it does not seed the Heavens for the rain which is yearned for. Your praise causes the formation of the cloud. Put this in your spirit. When ministers go into a service, they must already have built their cloud. They either prayed or praised it into existence. If we expect someone else to create our cloud for us, it will not work. It is not our cloud.

****

"If the music is live, then there is a praise inside of you that will bring the Glory cloud realm."

****

There is a cloud of healing and a cloud of prosperity. There is a difference between the cloud of Glory and the anointing. A few are healed when one ministers by the anointing in the word of knowledge. When the Glory cloud is present, the Heavens are open, and everyone receives. Always participate in the praise and worship time. Be part of the formation of the cloud. If you are part of the forming of the cloud, you know how to flow in the cloud. You cannot assume the formation. You have to be part of it. Why are clouds created? There can be no rain without clouds. There will be no clouds without praise.

All too often those in ministry arrive long after the worship has begun. What is more important than worshipping with the corporate body? If the head of the house arrives after the corporate body has ascended in worship, then the leader is not truly in tune with what is going on in the service. Herein lies an opportunity for the enemy to stir up problems. You have a worship leader who is in the realm of worship. He is hearing what the spirit is saying and is in tune with what God wants to do. Since the pastor is not in the service, the weight of responsibility weighs heavy on the worship leader. Then the pastor enters with his own cloud, which is not conducive to the cloud in the house. The results are more like thunderstorms than the soft patter of rain showers. The spirit might have been revealing truths into the body for that moment. While those in the service are hearing the message the spirit is saying, the pastor has been handling other matters, and the result is that it robs him of the ability to be in the flow of the anointing in the service. This is often why the minister goes away unfulfilled after a service, all the while thinking that something went wrong with the service, when in fact they did something wrong. They failed to be in unity with what the spirit was planning for that moment in time. They failed to be in the corporate ascent.

I have seen this scenario far too many times. The pastor walks out ready to preach his sermon. He senses that something is different about the atmosphere, but for the life of him cannot understand what it is. The worship leader has been wondering all the time where the pastor is. He knows that God is doing something, and because he knows his place, he is waiting for the pastor. In the midst of the questions, Lucifer has the opportunity to lie to both the pastor and the worship leader. There is not enough room here to list all the lies he places in their minds. But we know that jealousy and territorial ownership are just two of the greatest tools he uses.

The unity is destroyed, the service has lost the Glory, and the people are left to wonder why the service did not enter the presence of the Lord. We need to learn that worship must take place with all the giftings in place in the house.

I implore you pastors and worship leaders to get together and go before the Lord to get the Word of the Lord for the house. There must be unity. If a worship leader cannot be in full support of the pastor, he should step down. If a pastor cannot abide the ministry of his worship leader, he should talk it over with the worship leader, and make the necessary changes. The real question must be asked here. Do you want a music director, or do you want someone with a ministry of music? To stifle a psalmist is to strangle the spirit in them. Some of us who have served as staff members in churches need to remind ourselves of how things were. Most people have vowed they would never treat their staff a certain way when they take the reins of the house. Yet, the surge of power often blinds us to this vow. Dual kingdoms in the house will cause nothing but wars and rumors of wars. A house divided against itself cannot stand.

If you are a pastor, or a worship leader, who has fell victim to this trap, kneel down before the Lord right where you are and ask Him to forgive you for failing to be the priest unto Him first and foremost. Ask Him to restore your priorities He deems supreme. Then offer up your form and repetitive programs on the altar. Allow Him to reinstall His design and plan in your spirit. Lay your flesh aside and let the Glory realm into the house. He has said His house would be a house of prayer, not a house of agendas.

Now that you have cleansed your body, soul and spirit you are ready to ascend into that atmosphere where He resides. Lift your hands to the Lord. Lift your voice. Create your own Glory cloud. In the cloud that you create is your miracle, your breakthrough, your prosperity. Give Him praise! Go a little higher! Worship Him! Worship before His face. Kneel down on his footstool and place your head in His lap and allow Him to sing over you, His Bride. Your worship will create the cloud of His presence and then He will come down in all of His Glory.

The river I saw flowing over the entire earth was available to all of God's people. God said that the current in the river was changing as new waves began to break on the surface of the earth. Our expectations are not to be from those old familiar waves, but from the ever-changing new waves He is sending to the earth. Change is the hardest thing for humans to accomplish. We like the comfort zone far too much. We must disturb our present.

God told me some will be deceived and will miss this new wave of God because they will say they have seen it before. There are seen and unseen obstacles in the river that could block the flow of the changing current. But, with God's help, it is possible to rise above these obstacles and embrace the new waves of God. A word of warning, it will require some changes in your theology, traditions and thinking. This will be your greatest struggle. To give up what we have been told is the way to do something, to change our mannerisms and methodology, is as alien to us as stepping out of a spaceship onto the face of the moon. We know we are standing on new ground, and we know how we got there, but we have no idea as to the technology of the craft which took us there, or the composite of the terra firma we are standing on.

The Glory is altogether new to us. We are more comfortable talking about the anointing, but the manifest Glory is another story. We are challenged to go where no generation has gone before. We have already been in His realm.

We were created there. Now, we must learn how to access it once again, and reenter its atmosphere. "Whom He foreknew" has more to it than what we might think.

Renny McLean

CHAPTER FIVE

There is a New Sound
in the Earth

*"As we survey all the evidence, the thought insistently arises that some
supernatural agency, or rather Agency, must be involved.
Is it possible that suddenly, without intending to, we have
stumbled upon scientific proof of the existence of a
Supreme Being?
Was it God who stepped in and so providentially
crafted the cosmos for our benefit?"*
-George Greenstein, Astronomer

We are always in a season of constant change. We have been told in the Word
of God that we can know the times and seasons, and this is expressly so of those
which are shortly before us as the culmination of time quickly approaches. Time
is constantly being consumed by the hand of God until He comes bodily in the
fullness of time.

*"And unless those days were shortened, no flesh would be saved, but for the
elect sake those days will be shortened."* (Matthew 24:22)

When you realize that eternity is invading time, the challenge is to enter into
that realm where the view of how God sees time versus ours is different, whereby
a compression of time occurs. In other words, as the eternal mind of God invades
the natural mind of man, man is able to see, and understand, as God does.

As eternity invades time, time is being shortened, demanding that more is to
be accomplished in less time before Jesus returns.

Even though twenty-four hours in a day is still our accepted measuring of a
day and night, the perception of time is much different of time 100 years ago. It

was not thought to be inconvenient to take a year to travel from one continent to another. Now, man gets frustrated when he cannot get someplace fast enough.

Let me remind you once again of the passage in Daniel 12:4 declares:

"But you, Daniel, shut up the words and seal the book until the time of the end. Many shall run to and fro, and knowledge shall increase."

With the breakthroughs in communication, science, computer technology, not to fail to mention Internet mail, online banking, online purchasing, and the modern inventions of microwaveable food products; and don't forget the ability we now have to get a package around the world in mere hours, if you want to pay the price, when in the past it would sometimes take years for a ship to carry the mail from one continent to another. So, what previously took one year to complete is now taking one month. What previously took one month, now takes one week. What previously took one week, now takes one day. What previously took one day, now takes one hour. Let me say it in this manner. While time is being shortened, the events taking place in that space of time are seemingly being compressed.

If we can agree that He has authority over all things, then would He not also have authority over time? Only He can manipulate time. He created it. It is subject to Him. If He wants to cause our days to fly by faster than we are used to, then He can do it. We will not actually notice it because we would still be counting each moment as having sixty seconds, when in His reality, the seconds would be in what I call relayed time. While God has the power to do with time as He will, we would only perceive it in the natural realm.

What I want you to truly grasp is that our perception changes when we enter the mind of God the Father, God the Son, and God the Holy Spirit. In the case of the person given six months to live, that period of time might seem to fly by, while with another person it might be a very lengthy amount of time. Perception is the key word here.

We are living in the period when the prophecies declared over the past 6,000 years are being fulfilled in a short span of remaining time. Every passage from the Word concerning the world, the church, and Israel, is coming to pass. What an exciting time to be living. We are the generation which will see some of the greatest manifestations ever seen in, and on, the earth.

It is apparent there is a shifting in the Heavens as well as on the earth. There is more revelation provided to the Body of Christ than ever before. We are blessed to have some of the most wonderful men and women of God, who are sharing fresh insights into the Kingdom of God on a day-to-day basis, but the Word still does not change, even though there are new voices declaring fresh insight.

****

*"There are anointings being released in the earth
today that are making a dramatic impact."*

****

In the past few years we have said farewell to some of the most wonderful foundational leaders in the history of the church. My dear friend, and wonderful mother in the Lord, Ruth Ward Heflin has gone on to her reward. Her revelations, messages and visions of the Glory of God called the Bride to rise to new heights in Him. Our dear brother Kenneth Hagin, who birthed a revolution of faith in the house of God, and challenged us all to believe for the impossible, is now rejoicing in Heaven. The great theologian Derek Prince, who was one of the great voices in the Charismatic Revival in the seventies, has slipped into the Glory realm. These are just a few of those who have served the Lord with such intensity their lives touched us in the most powerful ways. But the message they preached and the mantles, which rested on them, have not been left in the dust. Others have taken the mantles and moved on to do even greater feats. I dare not begin to list these mighty men of God, lest I leave out one of them. So many of the great leaders of our day have laid foundations on which those who are answering the call to enter the work of God can stand on, and trust. Even as so many of them have received the mantles of those they sat under, there is a lineage of mantles from which all these mantles have come from.

There are anointings being released in the earth today that are making dramatic impact. These impacts remind me of the mantles carried by the giants, so to speak, within the Old Testament. We are seeing the fulfillment of the types and shadows of Elijah, Daniel, David, Samuel, Elisha, Moses, Aaron, Melchizedek, Ezekiel, Haggai, Isaiah, Amos, Solomon, Abraham, Isaac, Jacob, Enoch and all the rest of the patriarchs, and matriarchs, which make up that great cloud of witnesses in the Heavens.

These mantles were types and shadows of the anointing to come in, and through, Jesus Christ by the Holy Spirit. Just as the mantles came upon the cloud of witnesses caused the bearer to speak to the governments of both Heaven and earth, such will be and is the case, for those baptized in the Holy Spirit and Fire with the anointing of Christ today and henceforth until He comes.

As the Ascension Gifts (Apostles, Prophets, Evangelists, Pastors and Teachers) arise in the midst of the Body of Christ, we will see the residue of those mantles in the sound of their voices, the manner in which they approach the issues facing the perfecting of the saints, and the preparation of the Bride of Christ. We are going to witness some of the most powerful anointings appearing in these last days. They are being released for such a time as this.

Can you imagine how strange some of the statements were in the Epistles of Paul to the churches? He was sharing fresh revelation with them straight from the throne room of Heaven. They had the Law of Moses, and the writings of the Prophets in their possession. This was how they knew they were hearing truth, because it correlated with the writing of the Prophets, and matched instructions in the Law. Still, what they heard was blowing their minds. They had never heard anything like what they were hearing. Even when Christ was walking among them, they heard words from Him which were foreign to their understanding.

To make matters worse, the Sanhedrin created a group of spiritual leaders who followed those who were preaching the gospel with a new political approach to keeping their influence felt. These so called "judaizers" would tell the new Christians it was all right to accept Jesus Christ as Messiah and Lord, but they should not do away with the Law. They reminded them that the Law had served them well, and that it too was part of God. So if Christ was from God, then they should accept that He was as concerned about them obeying the Law as He was them accepting Him as their Lord. It was a great psychological ploy by the Sanhedrin, and I am certain there were thousands who liked the aspect that they did not have to betray their beginnings. But the truth was that those newborn Christians were in worse bondage as they attempted to live between the two worlds of the law and the grace offered them by Christ's teaching.

In these last days, the church will have a prophetic political voice unlike no other period in the history of this planet. The governments of the earth, through the crises and circumstances that are now being experienced, are going to turn to prophetic counsel as never before.

The Word of God in Amos 3:7 (NKJV) tells us, "Surely the Lord God does nothing unless He reveals His secrets to His servants, the Prophets."

God is raising up prophetic ministries never previously seen on the earth. The earth is witnessing priest-king relationships as in the day of Moses, where the prophets of the Lord walked into the house of many Pharaohs declaring the Word of the Lord. In this hour we will witness this same type of administration. It will be the Word they speak, coming forth as fire.

In one of our meetings the Glory of the Lord fell so mightily, and the prophetic word came forth as follows:

"For the atmosphere will change, says the Lord, and people will see Me in unusual ways. For it will come to pass, I will move through the prophetic voice with a sign and a wonder. It will shake the Heavens where they speak, it will shake the politicians. It will bring many of them to their knees. There will be many midnight conferences where the prophets will declare the Word with such accuracy that some will attempt to destroy the prophets because of their visions. And it will be a shaking like you have never witnessed. In that day, the voice of the prophets will rise above any other voice. The prophets will not speak counsel only; they will speak correction, rebuke and judgments. The fear of the Lord will befall on many kings. And these kings, because of the fear of the Lord, will cry out with a loud voice for the Word of the Lord. The Word of the Lord will become rare as cabinet members attempt to bring reason. The Word of the Lord, which came to the kings through prophetic utterances, will cause words of reasoning to fall to the ground. For it shall be, says the Lord, as I say, I will do. For the mouth of the Lord has spoken this."

Man's original state was void of circumstance as we know it because of the Glory in which he lived. This little parcel of Heaven on earth was called Eden. One of the meanings of the word "Eden" in Hebrew is "a moment in time". When God made man, He placed him in one of these moments in time. Paul, the apostle, said there were times he was "between and betwixt". He seemed to be in and out of both worlds at the same time. He stepped into the world that simultaneously exists with the eternal, or supernatural. As we enter into the

Glory cloud, we also can experience what the Apostle Paul did. What an exciting possibility!

The Scripture speaks of Jesus when it says, *"Who being the brightness of his glory, and the express image of his person, and upholding all things by the word of his power,"* Hebrews 1:3. Also as Revelation 4 states in verse 11: *"Thou art worthy, O Lord, to receive glory and honour and power: for thou hast created all things, and for thy pleasure they are and were created."*

Imagine, if you will, a day without worrying what time it is. Imagine having the ability to summon the animal kingdom together, and while they all sit before you, you give them their names. From that moment on, the animal knew who he is. Imagine walking through the garden, naming each flower and plant life all around you. In the cool of the afternoon, you walk and talk with God. You do not have a lack of intelligence to do so, as you have one hundred percent brain capacity. In fact, you are able to understand the supernatural as if it were natural. This is the result of the full impact of the DNA of God in you. What an incredible existence. Everything Adam did was to give pleasure to God by addressing the creations of God. This was the first praise and worship ever experienced in the earth. Man was excited about the things God created. The delight of them came in this manner. By drawing attention to those things God created, proclaiming those things glorious and wonderful, Adam and Eve were able to experience what no other creature could— perfected worship.

Worship brings us into the third Heaven. We worship Him in total Spirit and truth. In worship, we experience the original atmosphere He intended us to be in with Him. In worship you are not concerned with the elements of matter. He becomes the matter you worship. He is the revelation of all matter.

"...Without him was not anything made that was made." (John *1:3*)

He is everything that is and is to be, all the while waiting for us to simply worship who He is. Here is where the church has stumbled off the path into spiritual darkness. Many are obsessed with those things He has created more than they are in the rapture of His presence.

Can it be we have lost the desire to be caught up in His presence? Has the anvil, upon which our existence has been forged, hammered us into the restricted atmosphere of the earth? Have we become easy targets for Satan and his horde of demons that our warfare has become weak and powerless? Miracles become easy when the things of the earth no longer matter and our focus is totally on Him. The priority becomes His presence. Then your needs become His priority. We have seen it time and time again, miracles happen without as much as a prayer. When His presence is beckoned, His Glory is desired, this is when we will see Him in all His Glory manifesting Himself in our midst. We have seen eyes opened, deaf ears have unstopped, the dumb can speak, the lame walk, and creative miracles abound when the atmosphere is Heavenly, not earthly, permeated with all that He is.

Miracles come with ease when we worship in Spirit and Truth. We meet the Creator in the atmosphere for which He intended us to live from the very beginning. Worship is a lifestyle created by the God of the Heavens. It is in worship that we fulfil our purpose for being created. Fulfillment of the will of God on our part is worship. A paradox, one begats the other because they are intertwined. If we come with a heart to praise and worship God, putting our agendas and programs aside, we can be assured He will show Himself in the midst of His people. If we fulfill His requirements, He will fulfill His purpose.

God wants to show the world that He is the great I Am and that there is no power likened to His. When we praise and worship Him, the greatest power available to those who believe and walk in the Spirit is at our disposal. The time has come for us to expect the unexpected, experience the unusual, believe the impossible, and witness the miraculous.

****

"Your worship will open the new sound in the earth."

****

This is the hour of His Glory. Nothing else will suffice. Only His manifested presence will satisfy the ever-deepening hunger in the Body of Christ. This hunger is of divine origin. This is what you may be feeling as you read this book. You may be hungering for His presence, when all the time you are accepting the mechanics that take place in Church. Yet your expectancy is still the manifested presence of God.

Your worship is the catalyst to bring about the satisfaction you are seeking. Your worship will open the new sound in the earth. It is His song. It is from His heart. The melody must resonate from the innermost man. As our worship intensifies, along with the sound of all those around us worshipping, the sound gains mass. As that mass of worship takes on more energy, it begins to lift the entire group of worshippers into another realm—the Glory Realm.

There is a new sound in the earth. It is not just the sound of the refrains of an old familiar song. It is the sound of the heartbeat of God. It is the sound of His voice as it rides on the praises of His people. Can you hear Him as He sings His new song to you? Get those spiritual ears open and hear the song of Heaven. Hear the new sound filling the earth.

There are realms of God's personality being revealed now that were not known five minutes ago. The angels are going around the throne revealing the revelations of God that they haven't seen before. They don't need to go backward or forward because they have eyes before and behind them. They are singing the word "Holy".

Revelations 4 is the manifestation of divine worship. Anyone can praise but not everyone worships. When we sing songs, we already know, they have only one dimension. Until you sing the new song, the realm of the Spirit has not quite yet entered the service. In your spirit there is a song that can take you there. Someone else's song may not take you there, but the song inside your spirit can take you there. If you have to read off a wall to worship, you do not know how to worship because it is coming from your head. It is common for a woman to ask her man, "Do you love me?" He has to be told to say he loves her. It is not spontaneous because it came from his head, not from his heart. You don't need to be told if it's real. There is a dimension missing from the service because we sing songs that are contemporary, carnal songs. We may sing songs that are spiritually glorious but then we go back to the contemporary songs. We backtracked and the Glory started to lift. The Glory lifted because it can't mix with the old.

There are times during praise and worship where you always begin in the known. But when we start the service in the new song— and end with the new song—there is no contemporary song. We stay in the new song because the new song is the prophetic word being sung. Every song has a rhythm, a melody, and a beat. When Adam sinned in the garden, the whole rhythm of the earth changed. The supernatural became different. When something supernatural happened, it was an event. The original man was made to live in this event. Music is the international sound of the earth. When people sing they are prophesying. Some people shoot themselves in the foot.

They tell you, "I heard this voice when the song was being sung." Until people begin to sing the new song there is a dimension missing from the service. The angels are going around the throne singing Holy, Holy, Holy! What is the new song? When God created Lucifer, you could tell he was an odd one out. He was made with music in him. He was the worship department of Heaven. But he was still the odd one by the very name God gave him.

The el in the Hebrew language is an abbreviation for "God, mighty, strong one, creator". Gabriel and Michael have el on the end of their name. Lucifer doesn't have the el on the end of his name. Even as beautiful as he was when God created him, there was no el—or God—in his name. God never gave him His name. Lucifer thought he had it all. He thought Heaven would suffer when he was cast out. He wasn't counting on the Holy Spirit being the standby. The Holy Spirit waited for him to fall. Inside the Holy Spirit were the new songs that Lucifer didn't know. Inside the Holy Spirit are rhythms and tunes and melodies that Lucifer would never know. When Satan fell, the first thing God gave the earth was the new song.

Why the new song? To cover the atmosphere and the rhythm of the earth that was taken over by Satan's demonic music. The new song is made of a beat, a rhythm, and a melody. What is a rhythm? Some things happen in the Spirit, but we just don't know it. A rhythm is a movement. Someone is being healed, delivered, and set free with that new song. The new song is the Word of God being sung. The rhythm is the movement. What is the beat? The beat represents the timing. What time does it represent?

Now faith is. The beat sounds out the time, even though time has no real definition when applying it to the situation. Now, if praise is an affirmation, that I am being healed, delivered, and set free, when I praise the Lord, then your praise affirms that God has already done it for you. The rhythm is the movement, and the beat is the faith. How do we get the harmony? When the Glory of the Lord comes there is no rehearsal. Anyone can get in on that song.

There are just seven major chords in music. When we sing the song of the Spirit, it fits in with an eighth chord, which is a minor chord. In this minor chord everyone can sing in harmony. In the tabernacle of David only minor chords were used. It was called Tabernacle Worship. David had four shifts in the tabernacle. The Bible says we go from Glory to Glory. So, the next tabernacle shift picked up where the previous shift or team left off.

It wasn't the same Glory. It was a different Glory. It went on from Glory to Glory to Glory. Through their worship they kept the presence of the Lord burning.

There were supernatural activities taking place twenty-four hours a day. The devil hates it when we step over into the new song. I was raised in a bit of the Church of God. One of the chief goals we had in the London church was to teach the new song, or to sing in the Spirit. It was a painstaking effort because some people maintained that you couldn't sing in the Spirit unless God tells you.

As you might guess, there was a big misunderstanding in the gifts of the Spirit and tongues. We had to teach that speaking in tongues was different from God giving you a word. A message in tongues and interpretation equal prophecy but prophecy is listed at the top. So prophecy is basically speaking it forth. There are times in the realm of the Spirit that we will prophesy, and we speak in tongues. People think you are giving the interpretation, but in reality, you had the word before you spoke. When you were speaking in tongues, you were building up your spirit to give the word. It's all God but we should realize that we can prophesy—just say it. There are times you don't need to stir up yourself for it. It's already there. God is waiting for you to say it. When we sing the new song in the now, God wants to frame the movement. When are you going to step over and sing? When you step over it's another dimension entirely. Your services will be as different as darkness and light.

Can you imagine the day when we worship, where every wheelchair is emptied, every blind eye is opened, every deaf ear opened, and every cancer-ridden body is healed? We are coming to that, but we must learn to tap into the eternal when we worship. When we worship God, the eternal becomes our reality.

God desires us to sing the new song of the Spirit. We must change our worship, or it will be business as usual. Jesus is not coming for a church that is doing business as usual. He's coming to the people who know how to usher in the Kingdom and touch the supernatural. Those who truly know how to worship have learned to sing in Spirit and in truth as second nature. There's a song within your spirit that is relevant to the flow.

"Yet a time is coming and has now come when the true worshipers will worship the Father in spirit and truth, for they are the kind of worshipers the Father seeks." (John 4:23) (NIV)

Renny McLean

CHAPTER SIX

The DNA of the Body of Christ

For the past several decades, the church has seemingly departed from the intimate experience of the supernatural. The apparent lack of signs, miracles, and wonders has produced such a vacuum that many have attempted to fill it with a myriad of intellectual calisthenics and self-centered, self-exalting promotion. All this does is reinforce the very reason for the void in the first place. And so many leaders are looking to the testimonials of other churches on which to base their model. All this does is to alienate the people from God even more.

I deeply appreciate what God has done in several strategic locations around the world. I have had the privilege of preaching in most of those settings which have produced books, music and harvest testimonials for those locations. But I must warn the leaders in the western church to caution themselves in this hour. We must not become cookie cutter ministries. Each one has been called in their uniqueness to do and be something that someone else cannot. It is the individuality in God's creation that is so wonderful to behold. Yet, we are finding so many leaders heading to the bookstore, or on the Internet, to find an idea to market their church, or a sermon idea to preach.

I can understand reaching out to resources for educational purposes, architectural design and even organizational structure. But to mirror another church, just because they have a successful testimonial of what they have accomplished, is to miss the entire purpose and plan of God. He wants to talk to you. He wants to give you His plan for your ministry. Lay aside the books you have read, the seminars you have been to, and get into a quiet place with God where He can speak His plan into your spirit.

His Glory is experienced only where He is present. Merely talking about Him does not substantiate His presence. We must worship Him. This means to hear and obey Him. The axis point here is the word "worship". It was why we were created. It is what He hungers for from us. He yearns for intimacy with us. Worship is the highest form of intimacy with God. Can you not begin to see the mystery of this hunger? Do not forget that He is returning for a Bride who loves His appearing.

When two people love each other, there is often no need to communicate verbally. A slight gesture is all it takes to convey the intent of what the one wants to communicate to the other. People who have been married for several years finish one another's sentences which is a sure sign of the one mind they share. If we are to have the mind of Christ, then we must be able to sense the Spirit communicating to us at all times. I am reminded of all the times I am on the road alone. And as I am thinking about my wife and children, it is so wonderful to suddenly hear my cell phone ring and hear from them. It lets me know that our minds and hearts are beating as one.

This type of love is what the Father is hungry for with us. He does not want a Sunday kind of love. He wants the twenty-four, seven kind of love. God so loved this world that He gave us His son. That sacrifice had purpose to it. And that purpose was to reinstate our communication with our Creator. And the more you communicate with Him, you will suddenly experience a hunger for more.

The deposit of God's Glory in man is the very thing that is the conduit that carries this hunger back to His throne. What is it that drives us to call on God for a miracle? What is it in all of us that cries out for the manifestation of the supernatural power and demonstration of the Glory of God? Can it be that the original imprint man received from his creator has some residual resonance, which is activated by the supernatural? If this is not the case, we must look to the intellectual arguments that man is a need-based creation. On both counts we have sufficient grounds for an accurate analysis. Man is a need-based creation. God needed him. He needs God. For many the reality of God has taken on many forms. For some, miracles are the agent of proof. Some need scientific wonders, while others are looking in every nook and theological cranny for a sign of God.

Man was created in the image and likeness of God. And we are now being transformed in Christ into His likeness through the process of sanctification by the Holy Spirit. Therefore, we must have some defined element of Him in us. Can it be that when the supernatural is made manifest there is a stirring of the eternal DNA?

In Colossians 1:27 we read the words, *"Christ in you, the hope of glory."* Did we not gain His DNA through the redemptive work of the shed blood of Jesus?

Without redemption, there is only one destination, would any part of God go there? It seems to me that there is less and less attention being given to those benefits of the sacrifice Christ made on Calvary. It is impossible to become a new creation in Christ without the spilling of His blood. The blood of Christ is the prima face evidence of redemption. Man does not change by just believing and making up his mind to accept God. Yes, man must accept His existence, declare that His Son is who He says He is, but it takes the blood to transform us into heirs and joint heirs with Him. No miracle of healing happens without the appropriation of what those stripes on His back won for us. There is an old song that has the lyrics in it which go something like this, "Oh the blood of Jesus, it washes white as snow." It is true! His blood is the cleansing fountain, the eraser of the debt of sin, and the seal of our hope of eternity.

Contemplate, if you will, the few miracles I've shared with you up to this point. Do you sense there is a wanting, a desire to be a different kind of individual?

You may be asking yourself, "What is this atmosphere these people experienced that causes so many miracles to happen all at once?" It is the atmosphere of worship. It is the abandoned interest in the deity of Christ, not His ability to heal. The sickness is not the issue. Here is where we miss the point in God. We continue to make a demand on His creative processes, when He has placed the ability in us to call those things which are not as if they are. Revelatory intelligence is the "common sense" of the supernatural. The believer holds the key to the door to His presence. It is worship. We must accept that there must be some action on our part which calls to Him. He has already promised He would never leave us or forsake us. He has promised us that we would be able to accomplish greater things than He did. But we are required to do something in order to get to that place where He already is. We must come into the realm where He is, in the Glory. Access to this realm happens when you worship. As you worship, He inhales your worship and exhales His Glory. In the very breath of God is where you will find the atmosphere for the miraculous, the supernatural. But it will come when your full attention is on Him, and not just your need.

We need to learn how to court the Holy Spirit. In our summits, we worship sometimes two hours, and sometimes longer. Some of the religious people who have attended our meetings have complained that we took too long to worship. They said they were too tired to hear the message after worshipping for that long. Amazing! How can you grow weary worshipping the Lord? If you are mimicking worship in your flesh, then you will become weary; however, if you are truly worshipping Him in the Spirit, you will not become weary. His yoke is easy, and His burden is light, and time is not a factor.

****

"We need to learn how to court the Holy Spirit."

****

Many of the great forefathers of the apostolic ministries learned how to court the Holy Spirit. A friend of mine was telling me about the first time he ever encountered Kathryn Khulman. He had been ushered into her backstage room before one of her meetings. When he walked in the room, he saw Kathryn with her face turned away from him. She was crying and worshipping the Lord. The words that came out of her mouth struck my friend so hard he had to kneel down in the room as he was aware something very sacred was happening. Then he heard Kathryn Khulman whisper to the Lord, "Oh Father, will you trust me one more time?" I wonder if we truly know how much more we would have if we had the full trust of God in our lives. After a few moments, Sister Khulman turned and looked at my friend and told him, "Honey, all He wants is all of you." At that point my friend was overcome by the power of God. All he remembers is that sometime later, he awoke and made his way into the huge auditorium where the service was already in progress. The platform is not the only setting for the acts of God to be played out on. That moment in time changed my friend's life. To this day he still speaks of those words he heard her say, "Oh Father, will you trust me one more time?"

May I be so bold as to ask you the question, "Can God trust you?" The more you obey His commands, the more you show how much you love Him, the more you show you are in Him, and He is in you. The more you're with Him, the more your heart and His heart are in tune and you are like Him. The more you are like

Him, the more His trust is in you. There are requirements to the process of achieving an intimacy with Him. Have you presented your body a living sacrifice, holy and acceptable to Him? Have you denied yourself and taken up your cross to follow Him? Have you yielded your mind, will, and emotions to His mind? The life you live now is in Him. Outside of Him, you are not truly alive.

If you are sitting here reading this book wondering why you do not have a more powerful ministry, a larger congregation, or a larger bank account, you might consider the trust factor He has in you. Consider the previous paragraph as well as the following comments.

In the Middle East, the shepherds learn how to care for the flock from their early days as a child. The son of a shepherd is not given the responsibility of an entire herd for his first mission. The first part of his training is when the Father begins to train the son. He does not give this responsibility to any of the other shepherds. He takes the responsibility for his son on his own shoulders. He is given one lamb to care for. He must learn how to nurture that lamb to full maturity. After he has mastered the knowledge of the lamb, he is given another, then another, until soon he has an entire flock to care for. It is all a matter of trust. The Father has to see if the son is able to be trusted with the lamb. What a wonderful day it must have been in the camp when the Father announces to all the family, and other shepherds, that his son is now a man who they could trust with their flocks. We may have faith in God, and even trust Him. But can He say the same thing about us?

Faith is a most unusual process. It is the highway of communication between God and man. When this dispensation ends, time will be no more. We will not need faith! We will have experienced the finishing of faith. Remember, He said He is the author, and finisher of our faith.

Faith supersedes and will always interrupt, or break, the natural occurrence of the law of time. This is the difference between a miracle and a healing. Miracles are immediate and healings are gradual. When we pray in faith and say, "I am going to be healed," we have put our healing off to a future event. The man of faith, who may be praying for us and believing for an instant manifestation, is speaking from the eternal realm where "now" is the setting. But in too many cases, because of unbelief we hear him in the realm of time. What we actually do is disconnect from the "now" and position our faith in hope. This is why we do not receive immediate healing. While the minister is looking in the "now" the person being prayed for is actually changing the picture. Do you remember the statement made by Christ, "As your faith is, so be it unto you?" The operative word here is "as". In other words, what is the condition of your faith? What is the setting of your faith? Are you in the "now" or are you in the future? Some people say, "I need a miracle," but we are actually thinking, "healing". A healing takes time, a miracle does not. A miracle is immediate!

We have such a wonderful Lord! He has given us the keys to the Kingdom in order to continuously accomplish for Him those things which He did while He was on the earth. Ministry is not as it was ten, or twenty, years ago. Most of us were scholars of the Word, and now we are birthing a generation who knows more about philosophy, psychology and pathology than the Word of God. Please do not take offense to what I am saying. I applaud those who are educated. We must have all of those gifts to handle this complex society we are faced with today, but there is still nothing higher than the written Word of God other than that written Word becoming revelation, or that it becomes a resurrection Word by the power of the Holy Spirit.

An older minister once gave his son a powerful pearl of wisdom. He told him, "Son, you cannot truly love the Lord without loving His Word. For His Word is actually God in text form." Words to live by. When we take, and I mean that literally, Him at His Word, we can expect the unexpected! When that Word becomes a living reality within us, it fosters the "Christ in you" that instills "the hope of Glory".

"Father, I ask you, in the name of Jesus Christ your son, to release the hunger for your presence in this reader, right now! Allow them the revelation of how to walk in your marvelous trust. Grant unto them the fullness of their yearning. Baptize and empower them so that they are full of your Holy Spirit, NOW! Change them from the old paths and teach them the new path. Make them new wineskins. Give them the strength of mind, will, and emotions to stay the course you have called them to. Let them not despise the days of small beginnings, for in them are the lessons they will need for the maturing of the saints in their care. Cause those influences which are holding them from accessing the Glory to be disassociated from them immediately. Fill their temple with the train of your Glory! And from

this moment on, never let them regret they have made the decision to be a cloud builder of your Glory. In Jesus name I pray, Amen!"

Renny McLean

CHAPTER SEVEN

The Heavens and
Those Who Inhabit It

"Life in Universe - rare or unique?
I walk both sides of that street.
One day I can say that given
the 100 billion stars in our galaxy
and the 100 billion or more galaxies,
there have to be some planets
that formed and evolved in ways very,
very like the Earth has, and so would
contain microbial life at least.
There are other days when I say
that the anthropic principal, which
makes this universe a special
one out of an uncountably large
number of universes, may not apply
only to that aspect of nature we
define in the realm of physics,
but may extend to chemistry and biology.
In that case life on Earth could be entirely unique."
-Carl Woese
Microbiologist from the University of Illinois

The Bible speaks of three Heavens. The first Heaven is the atmosphere around the earth. The second Heaven is the atmosphere where Lucifer and his fallen angels were assigned to exist, between the third Heaven and the earth. The third Heaven is where we find God's throne room. This is where the Glory of God dwells. This is where we originated. This atmosphere is where we long to be, because it is where we came from. When we get hungry for the presence of God, we are actually homesick for the atmosphere He created us in.

At present, the earth is on a collision course with the eternal. The Bible declares that the earth will be filled with the knowledge of the Glory of God, as the waters cover the sea. The Glory of God is contained in the third Heaven.

Therefore, for this atmosphere to be poured out upon the earth, the distance between Heaven, and earth, has to be shortened in order for earth to be affected by Heaven's Glory. First, the earth will collide with the outer sphere, or the first Heaven. This is currently taking place.

As the first Heaven impacts the earth, time upon the earth is accelerated in anticipation of the third Heaven's Glory being poured out. Then, a collision with the second Heaven will cause the rupturing of demonic forces of evil, which will produce catastrophic events upon the earth, marked by what the Bible calls "end time events". Jesus warned of these events.

There are ten signs which define this period.

"And he said, take heed that ye be not deceived: for many shall come in my name, saying, I am Christ; and the time draweth near: go ye not therefore after them. But when ye shall hear of wars and commotions, be not terrified: for these things must first come to pass; but the end is not by and by. Then said he unto them, Nation shall rise against nation, and kingdom against kingdom: And great earthquakes shall be in divers places, and famines, and pestilences; and fearful sights and great signs shall there be from heaven." (Luke 21:8-11)

This is where the static interference between the throne room and the earth occurs, making open communication with Heaven more difficult than it was before the fall. For this reason, we see through a glass darkly. Before the fall, Adam could see clearly into the realm of the Glory of God.

The Apostle Paul speaks in 2 Corinthians 12:1-4 of being caught up to the third Heaven. "It is not expedient for me doubtless to glory. I will come to visions and revelations of the Lord. I knew a man in Christ above fourteen years ago, (whether in the body, I cannot tell; or whether out of the body, I cannot tell: God knoweth;) such an one caught up to the third heaven. And I knew such a man, (whether in the body, or out of the body, I cannot tell: God knoweth;) How that he was caught up into paradise, and heard unspeakable words, which it is not lawful for a man to utter. In so doing he was caught up into the Glory and into the future.

The future is up, not somewhere before us in this earthly time zone. Man thinks horizontally. As God manifest vertically, the impact issues out horizontally. Our future is in the Glory, in the Heavenlies, where everything comes from. If we would learn to think eternal, walk and talk as we truly were intended to, our existence on this earth would be so different as we know it. We are to have the mind of Christ. That means we are to reason, or think, as He does now. What a mind-blowing thought!

Can you imagine thinking light, animals, plants and even mankind into existence? And yet, the Word says that this is the creative mind we are to access daily. The resource is there. All we have to do is learn how to use it. And since we have not seemed to learn how to do so in the setting of the church at this present time, could it be that we have missed some vital part of the equation as to how to access that supernatural intelligence?

Our future is in the Glory. To put it in another way, our future is up, in a literal sense. Some of us prefer to look through a spyglass in order to see the future, when in reality all we need is the magnifying property of faith to see into the Glory.

Actually, the best time to get our spiritual sight is while we worship. We need to be caught up in worship in order to be able to see our future. God knew we would have problems on this earth, becoming distracted with what is going on around us. For that reason, He designed in us the capacity to worship Him. When we are truly centered on Him, everything else becomes clear around us. But our position changes when we worship, and that is what I really want you to place into your spirit. We are up there with Him, even though we are down here. We are seated with Him in Heavenly places, but we are actually standing on the earth. Or are we?

His solution was to give us wisdom, visions and revelations concerning the future in order to bring us up into a high place so we can look down from the realm of eternity into time and understand the end from the beginning.

****

"Our future is in the Glory."

****

What is up there, in our future, has always been there. We lack the understanding of how to grasp these mysteries and bring them into our experience now. There is a deposit, much like a bank account, in the Glory with your name on it. It is laid up for you in the Heavens. Accessing it is much easier than you would ever imagine.

Some say, "You are talking down to me." If we are trapped in this earth's time zone then in one manner it is so. If we access the eternal realm, and begin to declare things, then we would be speaking from "up" to "down". If we have laid up treasure in Heaven, where our heart is, and where we have originated from, then why do you think it impossible to access the account you have there. God has already given us the compound interest rates of Heaven. They are up to one-hundred-fold return on our investment. The key in investing in the Kingdom is to not confuse investing with seeding. Seeding is to prepare a harvest in order to invest. If all you do is look at what you do as seed, then you cannot recognize harvest when it comes. And if you cannot recognize harvest, then how will you recognize a Glory opportunity when God presents one to you?

Proverbs says to get wisdom and understanding. To know wisdom and instruction, to perceive the words of understanding; to receive the instruction of wisdom, justice, and judgment and equity; in fact, it calls it as valuable as precious rubies.

A dear friend of mine was relating his visit to the city of Heaven. Here is what he shared.

"On one of my visits to the Heavens, I was walking on the large boulevard which is in the central section of the city. Standing on this beautiful street formed out of the most incredible golden matter imaginable, I could look up and see on both sides of the streets the storehouses of God. As I entered into one of them, it was full of the most beautiful tapestries I had ever laid my eyes on. When I looked up it seemed there was no roof to the building. And there was too many bolts of material for me to even imagine. As I walked into another storehouse, it was full of golden vessels of all manner—pitchers, cups and saucers, plates and dining utensils of the most

exotic design one can imagine. I suddenly understood that all this was mine to use at my discretion. All I had to do was to ask Him!"

There was so much more I could share here, but the point is this; He still owns the cattle on a thousand hills! He owns all the gold, all the silver, all the bronze! He is lacking nothing in His Kingdom. As His child, and joint heir, we have a right to all of it.

CHAPTER EIGHT

Eternity!
Where Faith Reaches

The Time Zone of God

*"I find it as difficult to understand
a scientist who does not
acknowledge the presence of
a superior rationality
behind the existence of the universe
as it is to comprehend a theologian
who would deny the advances of science."*
-Wernher von Braun
(Pioneer Rocket Engineer)

Faith is the time zone in which God dwells. It is, it was, and it is to come. Faith is a higher law than time. It permits us to live, and operate, in that higher law. Through faith, we can access out of time into the eternal. Faith is the bridge, or passageway, the connection between time or eternity. Without faith the apprehension of an entrance into the eternal realm by the Spirit would not be possible.

We are often crises oriented, meaning that we do not perceive, sense to see, the Glory of God because we have conformed to the sense realm in which our crises exist. This type of perception or complex makes what we are actually seeing complicated with intellectualism and fact, not truth. Faith operates from, by, and in the law of truth.

He is the same yesterday, today and forever. He always is, and He always will be. He is God. God has always had problems in dealing with humanity, in that He is reaching from the eternal realm into a limited realm of time and space. In this respect He speaks a language we cannot understand. He knows this, but we don't. We are unable to relate to eternity from within a time realm.

How could this gap be bridged? It was up to God to take the initiative and solve this problem of communication failure. It would require a key to decode His thoughts, something that would work in both realms. It had to be a valid medium of exchange in the realm of eternity and the realm of time.

He provided a medium of exchange, valid in Heaven and on earth when He gave us faith. Faith is the currency, or gold standard, of the eternal realm, and also an honored currency, or standard, in the earth. God had to give man faith in order to elevate him above the constraints of time, space and matter so that man could have an intelligent relationship with His Creator.

The fallen mind of man cannot understand the eternal realm, nor grasp the fact that he was created for a higher dimension than what time, space and matter would determine for him. The human mind can hardly conceive that he has been given the key to subdue and change his predetermined boundaries set by time and space. The key is faith.

God gave us the gift of faith to open the prison door of time and escape, and freely access His glorious realm. The door swings both ways, giving us access to Him, and God direct access to us, without the limitations of doubt. Once the faith key is turned in the lock of time, nothing is impossible to man. He can then freely access the treasures of His loving Father.

Unencumbered by the weight of disbelief, we can then enter freely into His presence. We no longer doubt what God said He would do or when He said he would do it. Time is no threat to such a one. This thrills God, as He finds access to such a heart and mind and for that one, nothing shall be impossible. God can be God in such a man or woman.

Unbelief will not rob such a one of the supernatural dimension— together, they can reveal what the New Birth is really supposed to be—God in Man, bringing the Kingdom of Heaven to earth, and enforcing Calvary's victory.

Habakkuk 3:3 says, *"God came from Teman, and the Holy One from mount Paran. Selah. His glory covered the heavens, and the earth was full of his praise."*

The meaning of Teman is "nowhere". So it can read "God came from nowhere". I know this is hard for us to wrap our minds around the concept that someone, or something, has always existed, but that is part of this wonderful mystery of God.

He always was eternal. Before the beginning, there was nowhere for Him to come from. This is why He had to create "the beginning".

Scientists tell us that an exploding star, which is visible to the earth, is an event which actually took place outside of earth's time zone 300 years ago. It takes 300 years for that event to register in our time zone and become visible!

We know, too, that when the light from the sun's heat reaches us, seven and a half minutes have passed. So the heat we feel on a summer day is a passed event, and stale.

"I have declared the former things from the beginning; and they went forth out of my mouth, and I shewed them; I did them suddenly, and they came to pass." (Isaiah 48:3)

Something is suddenly about to rock your world. Something suddenly is about to shift in your finances. Something suddenly is going to move in your body. Something suddenly is going to move in your children. Something suddenly is going to move in your marriage.

We are in the season of sudden events! When you are at the point in your life when you cannot wait anymore, you are about to enter the sudden season for your life! Praise God ahead of the manifestation—do not wait to see it to believe it. Praise the Lord in advance of the miracle. Sudden debt cancellation! Sudden deliverance from years of oppression! Sudden promotion on the job! Expect it!

In order to understand the full manifestation of faith we must understand the constraints governing the dimension of time. If you hear or see through the veil of time, you are hearing and seeing through the veil of the curse. We cannot understand faith from a time standpoint. We cannot understand time from time. We can only understand time from the faith realm, which supersedes the time realm. We can only see a lower realm from a higher realm.

We cannot see a higher realm from the lower realm.

We cannot understand the operation of this fallen world by viewing it from the fallen perspective. We have to be taken into a higher place to get a vantage point. This is how we should view time, from the realm of the eternal. We cannot view the eternal realm from the position of time, as it makes no sense.

Faith has a witness to the Word. Look at how Mark 16:20 (KJV) speaks of faith.

"And they went forth, and preached every where, the Lord working with them, and confirming the word with signs following. Amen."

God identifies with faith, because faith and God are related. Faith is victory at work.

"For whatsoever is born of God overcometh the world: and this is the victory that overcometh the world, even our faith. Who is he that overcometh the world, but he that believeth that Jesus is the Son of God?" (1 John 5:4-5)

We must have the faith of God, not just trust. Trust is much like telling a child to jump from the side of a pool and that you will catch them. Faith is much more than trust. It teaches that even though you cannot see it in the natural, there is evidence to support that you will be caught. A child may trust the words, but to actually jump from the ledge of the pool takes faith.

Jesus came as the revelation of faith. He is the title deed of faith.

Hebrews 11:1 declares, *"Now faith is the substance of things hoped for, the evidence of things not seen."*

The Hebrews read from the right to left, enabling us to understand God always declares the end from the beginning and the beginning from the end. Hebrews 11 begins with the word "now". But what happened before we got to the now? The things which are not seen, or the eternal, calls out to evidence. Evidence calls out to hope, then hope calls out to substance. When substance appears, we can then declare the now. The "now" is supported by the evidence which has manifested.

Miracles are people related. By faith, actions of people activate God's response. Without faith, works are dead. Someone can believe for a miracle without having faith. Nothing will happen. The act of faith is what stimulates the miraculous of God. It is like the sparkplug in an engine. When the starter sends a charge to it, it responds by igniting the gasoline inside the engine.

****

"The life is in the blood."

****

Faith is a covenant action on the part of both parties. Every covenant was birthed through blood. Blood means life force. The reason why God's life is not understood is because we have not fully examined the meaning of the blood. When you hear the reference made to the life being in the blood, it is true. If you lose your blood, you lose your life. There is a phrase medics use when they are dealing with someone who has been shot or cut on a main artery. They say they are concerned with them bleeding out. What they are actually saying is that they are concerned with the life force bleeding out. The life is in the blood. So, when we apply this concept to the spiritual, we must realize that all that is in God is in His blood. It is His life force.

Everything God was, is and is to come is contained in the blood of Christ. Our faith is all too often blind to the hidden things of God. We rely on our faith, which is limited by our fallen intellect. Man often will rely solely on what he can see, hear, taste, touch and smell. God can manifest Himself in all of those realms and does. But when we approach faith through these five sensory realms, we are actually governing the amount of response we will accept from God. He works through more than just our sensory realm. The soul is the seat of the mind, will and emotions. If all we ever do is to interact with God in the soulish realm, we will miss out on what He is doing in our spirit man. The supernatural is where He manifests from, and that is only discerned from the spirit of man, not the soul.

When will we ever get to the place where we accept the reality that everything in Christ is ours? Did He not say that we are joint heirs? Are we not adopted into sonship? If so, then why would we settle to live through our mind, will and emotions and not His mind, will and emotions?

Now, when Jesus was walking the earth, He lived by, and operated, in faith. This is the faith covenant. The dictionary defines covenant as follows: "A binding agreement made by two or more persons or parties; a compact; contract. A solemn agreement or vow made by members of a church to defend or support its faith and doctrine. Theology. God's promises to man, as recorded in the Old and New Testament". American Heritage Dictionary.

So, if Jesus came to earth operating in faith, there must have been some vow, or agreement, from the Kingdom of Heaven concerning its faith and doctrine on which He was able to administer His declarations from. Without a legal vow or binding contract with the Father and the Holy Spirit, Jesus would have been acting illegally, or own His own. Since they are one, that was an impossibility. This makes the faith of Christ one that you and I can trust upon. It is a solemn agreement that we have entered into as His bride, and on His side of the agreement He has signed it in His blood. All that is required on our side is the faith in Him that He has won for us.

The very nature of God is faith. The character of God is faith. That is how we must view Him! When we revert to the fallen intellect of our Adamic nature, we miss out on so much of the covenant intellect He placed in us at salvation.

Now faith must become our life, because it is the evidence that God resides in us. The natural man is the outlet for the spiritual man. If the spirit is leading us, the flesh will follow. If the soul is in the lead, then the mind, will and emotions will be in the lead. Faith is a matter of the spirit. You cannot put faith in God's ability unless you know what His faith is. God is endless, He will always be. Regardless of the revelation you have, no matter the measure of it, you can put your faith in Him. He cannot fail. It is impossible for him to do so. God would not be God if He was a human. Humans are time leased beings. God is the I Am. We are in the I Am through Christ.

Mature faith does not give out in the middle of the process. There is a well-worn phrase I hear a lot in my adopted home state, Texas. The phrase goes like this, "You can't change horses in the middle of the stream". The reasoning behind this old cowboy statement is one which calls for experience. First, if you are riding a horse and you come to a stream, get to other side before you change to another horse or you might land in the water, or worse yet, get your boots wet. If you are in the middle of a river on a horse, the horse will allow you to get off him, but the other horse you might try to mount will not let you. He is already working on getting to the other side, and he is not about to take on more than he started with. It takes mature faith to see something through to its fulfillment.

Can you imagine where we all would be if Christ would have decided while they were trying him in Pontius Pilate's Hall that he had had enough. He could have just called on the Glory realm and left them all wondering where He went.

But! His faith was birthed in Him from His Father. His Father's faith was eternally matured. It always completed whatever the task was. Or can you imagine the Holy Trinity deciding during creation that on Thursday they had used all their creative abilities up? Absolutely ridiculous to think that they would run out of ability, isn't it? So why do we think we run out of faith when our faith is derived from Him? His vastness is our vastness.

Here are some nuggets I want to drop into your spirit man.

1. Receiving is the evidence of faith.

2. 2. The manifestation of what you receive is always current with what God is doing at that moment in time

3. The things that God wants to impart into us is His desires.

Because of these three elements, we are often found to be in spiritual warfare. The enemy would love to block us from receiving the evidence of faith. He would love to distort the manifestation, making us confused as to what we have received from God, and questioning whether it is from Him or not. When we find that our desires are actually creating a positive reaction in us, we all too often think that can't be possible! Why is it so hard to remember that He said He would give us the desires of our heart? And if our heart is like His heart, then the issues of our desires will match His.

The purpose of His blood cleansing our hearts is to allow faith to operate through the blood covenant. He actually purifies the blood, making it capable of carrying His attributes. The cleansing of His blood washes away all fear, doubt and unbelief.

You may be reading this and saying to yourself, "But why does my faith not work like this?" Faith is hindered by sin. When sin is present, it dilutes our faith. It is much like a viral infection. Even though the body is still able to function, it is not operating on the whole of its potential. This is the same when faith is being hindered by sin.

Faith counts everything done, finished and completed. Faith is not troubled by problems. Do you remember the story of Abraham found in Romans 4:19-21?

"And being not weak in faith, he considered not his own body now dead, when he was about an hundred years old, neither yet the deadness of Sarah's womb: He staggered not at the promise of God through unbelief; but was strong in faith, giving glory to God; And being fully persuaded that, what he had promised, he was able also to perform."

This was mature faith if ever there was mature faith. Abraham was over one hundred years old, his wife had a barren womb, and yet there was this vow, this agreement, this covenant which time could not alter. The purity if the vow empowered the promise. Abraham did not rely on his flesh to decide if the promise would be made manifest or not. The Word of God says he did not consider his body dead. Most men at that age will tell you they are as close to being dead as any person on the planet. But that is a time based statement, not a covenant declaration. Abraham must have been the model for the saying, you are as young as you think!

We have been given a faith covenant because God is a faith covenant God. He manifests through us, and to us, based on our relationship, not our association. Whatever you have faith in, that is what you believe. I have seen more men of God have more faith in the organization, mentors and denominations than they do the Creator of the Universe! Even Jesus had to rebuke the religious leaders, the Pharisees and Sadducees for not recognizing, or acknowledging who He was. "O ye, of little faith!" Even the disciples lived up to the same scrutiny. Modern religion makes more about their programs, philosophy, rules, regulations, and association responsibilities than they do the things of God. And the entire debate is over faith!

****

"Tell them it is the faith of God in Christ Jesus."

****

When people on the street come up to you and ask you what is your faith? Tell them it is the faith of God in Christ Jesus. But for goodness sake, don't respond by telling them what denomination you belong to! The last thing they want to hear is your dissertation on your doctrine on faith. They are asking the right question, so don't give them the wrong answer.

If the Kingdom of God were a television network, faith would be the satellite dish we use to pull the signal out of the airwaves. When television was in its infancy, it was in black and white. The picture was not quite as clear as today's high definition, but it was a marvel to the world all the same. Much like the early days of the church, a great deal of what was heard and seen was like our old black and white televisions. As we grow closer to the coming of the Lord, knowledge has increased, and we are now seeing and hearing a much different signal. The signal is getting stronger as we approach the actual realm from which the signal is originating. As eternity invades time, the signal intensifies. In fact, there is a tremendous amount of receivers sounding out the message of these changes occurring in the earth and the Heavens.

CHAPTER NINE

Dominion Over Time

"Then we shall be able to take part
in the discussion of the question of
why it is that we and the universe exist.
If we find the answer to that,
it would be the ultimate triumph
of human reason - for then
we would know the mind of God."
-Stephen Hawking
British astrophysicist

Time was created. God gave man dominion over every created thing, including time. In the Genesis account of creation, we see where time came into being on the fourth day. It was created by cosmic light and did not always exist on this planet. Time finds its definition by virtue of days, months, seasons, and years, all the result of the revolving of the earth around the sun, and the revolving of the moon around the earth. Without the revolving planet system there would not be a calendar, and no way to measure our days, nor could we judge our age.

"When I consider Your Heavens, the work of Your fingers, the moon and the stars, which you have ordained what is man that You are mindful of him?" (Psalm 8:3) (NKJV)

"You have made him to have dominion over the works of Your hands..." (Psalm 8:6) (NKJV)

Since time is created, it is included as "work of His hands" and qualifies to be in subjection to those whom God gave dominion over this planet. Time, like money is to be our servant, not our master, but if we do not know how to exercise our God-given dominion over it, it will rule over us as a cruel taskmaster. We need to understand the operation of time and eternity in order to master our dominion in this realm. Not until we understand the workings of time and eternity can we ever really understand faith, as faith was given to man to manipulate time. Faith is a dominant force, given to man to rule over time, as real faith says when it will happen, and time must bow to that decree.

We understand in modern science that, in fact, it was the earth that stood still, not the sun, but the effect was the same. Time was held ransom for 24 hours until man declared it could resume.

Here's an interesting excerpt from an email that has been circulating for a couple of years. There has been some question as to the validity of this story, so I will allow you, the reader, to make your own judgment here. If this story is not true, the basis on which the tale sits allows us to use this as a wonderful illustration of how science might react to the use of their abilities to look into the Heavens and read the story set forth by the hand of God in the firmament.

The story goes something like this. A Mr. Harold Hill, the presumed President of the Curtis Engine Company in Baltimore, Maryland and a consultant in the space program related the following development.

The astronauts and space scientists at Greenbelt, Maryland were checking the position of the sun, moon, and planets out in space where they would be 100 years, and 1,000 years from now. "We have to know so we won't send a satellite up and have it bump into something later on in its orbits. We have to lay out the orbits in terms of the life of the satellite, and where the planets will be so the whole thing will not bog down," they exclaimed. They ran the computer measurement back and forth over the centuries and it came to a halt. The computer stopped and put up a red signal, which meant that there was something wrong, either with the information fed into it or with the results as compared to the standards. They called in the service department to check it out and they asked, "What's wrong?"

Well, they found there is a day missing in space in elapsed time. They scratched their heads and tore their hair. There was no answer. Finally, a Christian man on the team said, "You know, one time I was in Sunday school and they talked about the sun standing still." While they didn't believe him, they didn't have an answer either, so they said, "Show us."

He got a Bible and went back to the book of Joshua where they found a pretty ridiculous statement for anyone with "common sense." There they found the Lord saying to Joshua, "Fear them not, I have delivered them into thy hand; there shall not a man of them stand before Thee." Joshua was concerned because the enemy surrounded him, and if darkness fell they would overpower them. So Joshua asked the Lord to make the sun stand still! That's right!

"And the sun stood still, and the moon stayed, until the people had avenged themselves upon their enemies. Is not this written in the book of Jasher? So the sun stood still in the midst of heaven, and hasted not to go down about a whole day." (Joshua 10:13)

The astronauts and scientists said, "There is the missing day!" They checked the computers going back into the time it was written and found it was close but not close enough. The elapsed time that was missing back in Joshua's day was 23 hours and 20 minutes— not a whole day. They read the Bible and there it was, "about (approximately) a day." These little words in the Bible are important, but they were still in trouble because if you can't account for forty minutes, you'll still be in trouble 1,000 years from now. Forty minutes had to be found because it can be multiplied many times over in orbits.

As the Christian employee thought about it, he remembered somewhere in the Bible where it said the sun went backwards. The scientists told him he was out of his mind, but they got out the book and read these words in 2 Kings that told of the following story: Hezekiah, on his deathbed, was visited by the prophet Isaiah who told him that he was not going to die. Hezekiah asked for a sign as proof. Isaiah said:

"Do you want the sun to go ahead ten degrees?" Hezekiah said, "It is nothing for the sun to go ahead ten degrees but let the shadow return backward ten degrees." Isaiah spoke to the Lord and the Lord brought the shadow ten degrees backward! (2 Kings 20:9-11) (NKJV)

Ten degrees is exactly forty minutes! Twenty-three hours and twenty minutes in Joshua, plus forty minutes in 2 Kings, make the missing day in the universe! Isn't it amazing? (References: Joshua 10:8,12-13 and 2 Kings 20:9-11)

No matter if this story has any validity to it, I am certain there are happenstances much like this one that take place all the time in the world of science. Unexplained phenomenon is an everyday occurrence, and yet we know it all to be possible in the realm of the supernatural.

Since time falls into the category of creation, it is no wonder that the earth stood still for twenty-four hours in biblical history at the command of Joshua. Therefore, man has the ability to subdue all of creation, including time.

Time was given to the Sons of Men. We are the Sons of God, born from another system where there is no time. God has put Eternity in our hearts. Eternity is the Glory Realm. We have to learn to operate from where we came, not from where we live presently in this fallen time zone. Faith was given to us by God to break the time warp where we become trapped. Unlike time, the eternal has always been, and was never created.

This Glory realm is our birthplace, and for those who are born from above by accepting the shed blood of Christ Jesus, it is our future home. However, time was created on the fourth day; it did not always exist. Through this created fourth-day light we have been given dominion, as contained in our original lease over this planet, which was given to Adam.

For us to receive our miracle—or to administer miracles in this earth—we need to understand our dominion over time. All those who operate in miracle ministries have learned how to subdue time and enforce the unseen world upon the seen world. No one moves consistently in the supernatural realm without understanding how to supersede time. If we don't learn how to supersede time, we're going to have to work with it, and feel its obvious constraints. We need to know there is nothing that God is going to do that He has not already done. The secret is we have to learn how to reach up into that world and bring it into the here and now.

John 11:1-44 gives us the account of Jesus raising Lazarus from the dead. We see however, when Jesus heard that Lazarus was sick, he could have left immediately, but did not. When he finally arrived at the house, Martha scolded Him for not being there, saying, *"If you had been here, my brother would not have died."* He replied that Lazarus would live again, and asked Martha, *"Do you believe this?"* He went on to say, *"Your brother will rise again."* She replied, *"I know that he will rise again in the resurrection at the last day."* She named the time that had her reality sometime in the future.

Although Judgment Day is a set day in the future, she had failed to realize that Jesus had come out of that day and came back to her day, saying in effect,

"Martha, you don't have to wait till that day." She didn't realize that the resurrection was not an event, it was a person. Jesus said, "I am the resurrection." Don't be constrained by your lack of understanding of time. Seize your portion right now! He was saying, "If you believe, you don't have to wait until that day!" He meant that faith could take you beyond time into the future to take your portion right now.

****

"What is revelatory to the Heavens is prophetic to the earth."

****

Those who don't understand faith are forced to wait for the date the doctor has set to receive their healing. If he had said six months, defy the law of time and activate the higher law of faith; reach into the future and take your healing right now!

What is revelatory to the Heavens is prophetic to the earth. Things in the Heavens are not learned, nor can they be. They are just known. It is not possible to study and learn the revelatory realm. It must be revealed. It is possible to learn the operation of the prophetic realm, but not the revelatory realm. There is a world of difference between the revelatory and the prophetic experience. They are governed by different rules, as the one originates from the throne of Glory, and the other originates from this fallen atmosphere. Heaven operates in present tense, while the earth has different time zones, or tenses. Here we have past, present, future, and future perfect tense. If anything comes to the earth from the Heavenlies it has to fit into one of these four tenses in order to remain in the earth and manifest in these three-dimensional realms. It has come into the earth, leave the realm of eternity from whence it came and penetrate the realm of time. For this to happen, it must be framed, or claimed by the words of our mouth. Then it remains in our time zone and will manifest to us in the natural realm.

Scientists have proven that the farther out we go from the earth, the farther we become removed from time. The distance between Heaven and earth is constantly changing. This is because the Heavens are moving toward the earth in anticipation of the rapture of the church and the day when the earth is renewed with the Glory of God. God declared that the earth shall be filled with the knowledge of the Glory of the Lord. This can only come from the Heavenlies.

The original distance between Heaven and earth today is not what it was after the fall. The two worlds are closer now than ever.

Deuteronomy 11:21 (NKJV) reads: *"That your days may be multiplied and the days of your children and the days of Heaven upon the earth."*

We see from this that God has intended for man to walk in Heaven's atmosphere right here on this planet. When one prophesies, he does not speak from time, but from Eternity. Everything is already finished in the Heavens, so there is no need for prophecy. Everything in the Glory is present tense, now knowledge.

There is no past, present or future in the Glory. Everything is complete and whole in the Glory. Prophecy is reserved for the earth, for the realm of time. It becomes a creative force, reaching into the future and bringing the future into the now. True prophecy never speaks from time, for it would then be distorted.

Prophecy speaks from eternity, for it sees the finished result of the declared word. A prophet will not speak from the present to the present tense. He will always speak from the future into the present tense. Prophecy will cease, but the revelatory realm of the Glory will never cease. This is because prophecy is reserved for this earth's time realm, where the future exists. In the Glory there is no future. Everything is present tense.

Second-day prophecy is different from third-day prophecy. Prophecy is about to change dramatically. As the two worlds collide, Heaven with the earth, time as we know it on this planet is being dramatically altered. Eternity is invading time, and time is being displaced.

Prophecy always ministers through time, so therefore prophecy is about to change as well. Because ministry gifts see ahead of time, God does not deal with prophets according to time. The vision of the prophet supersedes time and space, mocking the devil's determination to keep man without hope and a future.

Paul saw the Great Cloud of Witnesses while in the Glory. When our saved loved ones die in Christ, they move up to join the cloud of witnesses cheering us on into our future. They are already in the future, and eagerly watch us as we seek to understand and lay hold of our future. We need to get up, out of this earth's gravitational pull which keeps us earthbound, in order to hear and see clearly and know what is to come. This information is only available in the Glory, once we break the bonds of time and look back from there. We get there by sincere prayer and worship to God. Time, which is in need of being redeemed for whatever reason, is always in the past tense, never the future tense. So God must take us back to the past in order to redeem the past. If He never redeemed time, we could never enter our future.

As a young man, while still living in London, I walked into a fish and chip shop one day for lunch. The atmosphere was tense in the shop, and a fight was on the verge of breaking out among squabbling customers. At the time I was doing a lot of body building, so at 6'2" and 270 pounds, I looked like a formidable opponent. Without even looking for trouble, I was pulled into the strife-filled atmosphere of the room.

Suddenly a man walked into the shop (a man much larger than me), and without saying a word got me out of potential harm. Instantly, when he was at my side, the atmosphere changed, and the natural order was restored in the shop. Everyone felt it, including the brawlers, yet no one understood who the man was or what had happened. Then he disappeared.

I knew he was an angel who walked into the scene, bringing with him the eternal realm, and restored the atmosphere back to its original order before I had entered the shop. In an instant, time was redeemed, and the clock set back to the original atmosphere, which existed before I ever entered the fish shop.

Christians have traditionally steered clear of anything they don't understand and cannot control. For the most part, the average Christian is trapped in this time-space warp, a world not native to the born-again believer. However, within every believer is placed the ability to access—and be comfortable in—the atmosphere God is comfortable in, which specifically includes the timeless zone.

Why then would we think it strange to explore the realms of space, time and matter travel? Is this dimension only for scientists? They can never fully understand the ramifications of time-space-matter travel without grasping the spiritual realities behind it: the realm of the spirit, and the realm of the Glory. Once we discover the fragility of time, it becomes obvious that the same laws governing time govern space and matter and are equally conquerable.

****

"In order to be translated, one must defy the laws of time, space and matter."

****

This is the realm that births miracles. It is also the realm where time-space-matter travel (or being translated) is born. In order to be translated, one must defy the laws of time, space and matter. Just as we see examples of men being translated in the Bible, so it shall become common in the Glory that is about to be poured out in the earth. We shall find ourselves standing on another continent, before crowds of people, with no understanding of how we got there, equipped with the supernatural abilities of God.

God is able to take us backward and forward in time. He took Moses into a high mountain and showed him thousands of years into the future to the church age. He took Isaiah into a high place in the Glory and showed him many different time zones. He saw events for his day, he saw the coming Messiah and the church age, and into the glorious church, or the third day church. In the Glory there is no time, so he was able to assimilate this information and move backward and forward in time, once he was lifted out of this earth's atmosphere where time holds us prisoner.

God is looking for "seers" in this day. These are people who are willing to get alone with the Almighty, those who will be willing to come into a high place in the Spirit and view the earth realm from a Heavenly point of view.

He desires to show His people what is to come in the immediate future and in the far distant future. In order for one to see, they have to be caught up—out of this time zone—to view it from the perspective of eternity. One cannot understand time from time, only from eternity.

God is able to take us backward and forward in time—back to the cross, forward to the future—thus conquering the dictates of this fallen time dimension. We were made to rule over time, not for time to rule over us. There is no such thing as miscommunication in the spirit world. When individuals are attuned to the same frequency, there is no possible way to "mishear".

Communication is very clear in the realm of the Glory. When one is hearing in the realm of the spirit, the communication is direct spirit-to-spirit. Miscommunication only comes about when one is hearing from this fallen, earthly time zone, where there is interference and sound is corrupted. The further from the earth realm one gets, the clearer the sound and the sharper the communication.

This applies to our communication with God and with one another. In the realm of the spirit sound changes because it is in its purest form. Interference comes from the second Heaven, where demon spirits dwell, trying to corrupt the communication that proceeds from the throne room of God to His children on the earth.

However, when we worship until there is an open Heaven, we are able to clear the Heavenlies and gain access to the Glory realm, where communication is clear and impossible to misunderstand.

The Bible declares that where two or three agree, it is grounds for a decree. By agreeing with the doctor's sentence of time, we establish it as law in our lives. Refuse to give any man the right to decree your life span. Believing a medical report that places a death sentence upon someone is no different than accepting the words of witchcraft in Africa or India.

If we accept a death report from a physician, our body clock will adjust to the words that have been decreed, and the death principle is set in motion. You will become preconditioned to respond to that word.

Only our Creator has the right to determine the length of our days. Agree with what His Word says about you and allow that to be the mediator between you and your ailment. Agree with the Word and allow that to be the grounds for a decree that shall stand in the earth and be upheld by the courts of Heaven. Faith calls six weeks, two months, six months or one year away from here, NOW. Faith calls it all NOW. It has no other response.

When we agree with faith, it brings something from the world beyond into our world and brings time to a screeching halt. Then, time sees that when faith comes on the scene it cannot go any further. By exercising our faith, God holds time ransom, just long enough for us to get our miracle now!

The key to accessing the creative realm of God is spontaneity. God is always creating. He has never stopped creating. Our spontaneous obedience to the prompting of the Holy Spirit causes us to get involved in the creative processes of God. When we obey God in our giving, we immediately change seasons from seedtime to harvest time. When we give by faith and not from time, we break the natural laws of time and cause our harvest to come from the future into the now. As long as you see time, you will never give to God what you have in your possession, because time reflects your situation.

Because time becomes the constraint and the determining factor in what you are able to give God, therefore 98% of our giving that comes into the work of

God is seldom given by real faith. Why? Because it is given from the realm of time. The only thing separating you from a billionaire status is time.

The world has adopted a deceptive comment; the phrase, "time is money". It sounds good, but the truth is, time is not money. Time is temporal. What God gives is permanent. When God created Adam he had everything, but when he sinned he lost his rights as legal heir to the riches of this earth, and it was only by the sweat of his brow that he could earn bread.

Whereas man was able to easily receive the riches of this planet in the beginning, after the fall there came a yoke and a burden attached to obtaining wealth. Now, the only thing that stands between our wealthy place and us is time.

The only thing that stops us from giving millions into the work of the gospel is time. Time becomes the mediator between our destiny and us. We think the natural process of time is required to work out in the natural and bring the wealth that we are to give. The laws of the natural do not govern us if we are truly in Christ Jesus! In the supernatural, what would take a year can now take a day!

I met a man in the ministry twelve years ago who lived in extreme poverty. During one of my meetings, this man was impressed to give generously into the offering. When he did that, the spirit of prophecy fell upon me and I told the man that he would shortly come into great wealth. Within six months a relative died and left this man a vast inheritance, worth millions of dollars in land value and cash assets. The man-made terrible mistakes that ultimately robbed him of his entire inheritance. First, he neglected to tithe to the Lord. In doing so, he failed to register this wealth in his own name in the Heavenlies.

****

"No man or woman of God ever walks into a higher realm with God, without first making a vow to God."

****

As a result of this, the wealth was never transferred into his name in the realm of the spirit. By tithing he would have sealed his inheritance and rendered the devil powerless to steal any of it from him. So it wasn't long before this man lost the whole amount and was reduced to abject poverty once again.

No man or woman of God ever walks into a higher realm with God, without first making a vow to God. There are certain things in the spirit which are inaccessible to us outside of us making a vow.

A vow is a solemn promise you will give to God.

That vow enables God to use the words of our mouth as credit, because a vow releases God to go into our future harvest and bring us a deposit out of that time zone into the now and bring it to us as operating capital for whatever the need.

Many people are in financial trouble because they never honored their vow. Things in the spirit become locked away until the vow is fully honored. When we do not honor our vows, we are in a state of bad credit with God, and God cannot take us at our word.

Our future gets cut short right there, and can no longer be attracted to us, however when the vow is honored, God's hand is released to access things from the future and brings them into the now. It is imperative that we learn how to attract and invite our future to us. If we do not, we will always attract our past. Your past is as close to you as your future.

We should learn to dress our future, and dress according to where we are going, not where we have been. When your future sees that you have dressed it, it will begin to come to you. Then when it comes to you, you are there. It does come to stand as a fact that if you cannot afford to dress like a millionaire, at least you can do the best you can do with what you have. Too many have felt defeated because they did not have the millions to do what they wanted to do, so they gave up believing that attaining their dream was possible. In and of yourself, that may be true, but with God, all things are possible. Let your future invade your present!

As written in the book of Malachi 3:3 (NKJV), *"He will purify the sons of Levi and purge them as gold and silver that they may offer to the Lord an offering in righteousness."*

Allow me for a moment to share with you a revelatory insight I believe will interest you, if nothing else it will make you sit up and take a second look at the refining fires of God's chastening. Gold has certain properties about it. For instance, The Atomic Number: 79; it's Atomic Radius: 144 pm; and the Atomic Symbol: Au. The Melting Point is 1064.18 °C while the Atomic Weight is 196.9665. And the Boiling Point is 2856 °C. The Electron Configuration used for Gold is [Xe]6s 4f 5d. All of this indicates that there is a process which takes place in the internal properties, as well as the processing of the gold to make it pure is an altogether different process. It takes massive amounts of heat to purify it. This should give us some idea as to what God meant when He speaks of fiery trials and us coming out as pure gold.

This is the year when the priesthood is being totally refined and purified, in order to offer pure spiritual offerings to God. Only a pure vessel is the fit for the Master's use and prepared to carry the Glory which is being poured out upon the earth at this time.

Corruption cannot contain the Glory. It is a dangerous thing to handle the Glory with unclean hands. It is the season where God is cleaning up the church, beginning with the Sons of Levi and continuing all the way through to the end time martyrs.

We cannot continue to walk in the old ways of religion. We must come out from among those who are satisfied to sit in the seat of the scornful, and the counsel of the ungodly. While Jesus walked this earth, He desired to have the revelation of the Heavens to become known to the people. In every parable He showed another side of His own personality, His own intent and origin. His heart was as transparent as glass, while His own friends had a problem believing that He was who He said He was. Take for instance the time when He walked into the Synagogue on the Sabbath. Now you must understand that what He was about to do was so prophetic, that not one in the Sanhedrin picked up on it. Instead, He incited a riot of religious debate.

Each Rabbi was assigned a day to read the Torah. On this day, it was Jesus' turn to read. It was His appointed time. The Lord stepped to the podium and began to read out of the book of the Prophet Isaiah.

Luke recorded it in Chapter 4:18-20:

"The Spirit of the Lord is upon me, because he hath anointed me to preach the gospel to the poor; he hath sent me to heal the brokenhearted, to preach

deliverance to the captives, and recovering of sight to the blind, to set at liberty them that are bruised, To preach the acceptable year of the Lord. And he closed the book, and he gave it again to the minister, and sat down. And the eyes of all them that were in the synagogue were fastened on him."

When He finished reading, He sat in the seat reserved for the Messiah. This is when the religious spirit of tradition wanted to kill Him. Anytime we find out the truth for ourselves, religion wants to destroy us. Anytime we find out that we are a prophet or something else that the organization doesn't recognize, they may take steps to put us down. Anything considered different is judged as an affront to the known truth.

Religion keeps a person trapped in their past, in order to keep them from attaining their future or destiny. Even the woman with the issue of blood challenged tradition. She even broke Jewish traditions when she moved among the people to get her miracle. If we are not prepared to break the traditions of men, we will never see miracles in the church. Considered unclean, she broke fourteen Jewish laws to touch Jesus. Yet most of us would not break even one because we are afraid of what people would say.

****

"Tradition destroys unity."

****

There are traditions that most of us are holding on to because it is all we have ever known. God is trying to rip them from our grasp. If you want tradition instead of truth, then the Word of God is of no effect.

"Making the word of God of none effect through your tradition, which ye have delivered: and many such like things do ye." (Mark 7:13)

Tradition destroys unity. Too often there is disunity in church leadership because some are birthed and steeped in tradition. They are not the Word made flesh. They are tradition made flesh. When something new comes along there is division. If and when there is division in the leadership, there is division in the anointing in the church. This is why people aren't healed and why the anointing goes over people, why at times there is no anointing and why at other times the anointing is not strong.

If the leadership does not want a move of God, then the move cannot stay in the church. Tradition often looks like this. The elders conspire together. They call each other and say, "We don't like what he is saying and doing. We have to get him out, but we will appear as if we are with him." When this happens, the man sent of God is preaching to two camps of people. There is no unity of the faith. The atmosphere for the miraculous is spoiled.

If the elders are not in agreement on what God is about to do, then changes in leadership are necessary. This is scriptural.

Amos 3:3 says, *"Can two walk together, except they be agreed?"*

Some of you may feel like the Jews leaving Egypt. You never thought it would happen, but the day has come. You are free at last. You don't care what man says, because, like Paul, you are going to say, "I have neither conferred with flesh and blood." (Galatians 1:16) What God has put in you didn't come from another man. You got it from the throne of God. You couldn't quit even if you tried. The greater is working in your circumstances. You are called. It is your destiny.

Take your stand and get into agreement with what God has planned for your life. We are living in the hour when that which was dead will live again. Come forth, Lazarus! Stretch forth your hands! There is an anointing that you used to walk in. There was something inside of you that you are not walking in now. Call it forth. Faith and calling, anointing, miracles, signs, wonders, come forth!

"I rebuke, bind, uproot and tear down every spirit of religion, tradition and unbelief that works against the plan of God in you. In the name of Jesus, I set you free. Lift your hands up and praise Him. You are loosed to be what God has called you to be!"

God is raising up a people to tear down the spirits of religion and tradition. The first thing God does when He wants to move on the earth is to break up the structure of man. Structure tries to contain God. It says, "This is how God is."

The Jews had Him in a cloud by day and a pillar of fire by night. They thought they had God in a box behind the veil. When Jesus died, God rent the veil and went public. They put the residue in a box and religion was born. This is a generation that won't accept the residue. We want something new; something fresh, and we want it now!

Renny McLean

CHAPTER TEN

Breaking the Laws of Time

Until we learn to break the laws of time, we will never walk in the supernatural. If God had intended us to live by natural time, He should have never given us faith! Faith is the key that dismantles time. Time has set itself up as a mediator between man and his dreams. Time determines our lives with unchallenged tyranny. Ignorant men and women feel helpless against a sentence of time given by a physician or waiting for deliverance of any sort. It has ruled our lives mercilessly. Convincing masses that it is an undisputed monarch. However, when the revelation comes to us of how fragile time actually is, and of how we can break its laws, we see how thin the veil really is. Once we break the laws of time, it becomes easy to break the laws of space and matter, as they are all governed by the same rules.

It is not difficult to see how time bows in the presence of a greater revelation of faith. Once we understand the operation of the dominion of time, and we gain the revelation of the higher laws of faith, we easily begin to see that time hangs its head in defeat. Time then is nothing more than a dethroned monarch. Dictatorship ends abruptly once its secrets are unveiled. Once this is accomplished, we can take off all those things which hinder our ability to fully commune with Him.

****

"Faith is no respecter of time, and time does not determine faith."

****

Faith is nothing more than the compression of time. Faith is governed by a higher law and operates on a higher realm than time. Therefore, it is the dominant realm to which time must submit. When faith declares when something will be, natural time always submits and produces the evidence as decreed by faith. Time will compress to make way for faith. Faith is no respecter of time, and time does not determine faith. Time seeks to subdue everything and everyone to its natural progression, imprisoning those who will conform to it. Only the laws of Heaven govern faith, as it comes forth from the Heavenly realm.

The force of faith is launched in words, like a missile from the mouth of the believer, to fulfill its task, and will conquer impossible barriers of time and space to get its mission accomplished. Therefore, faith is the ability of God in us to superimpose the invisible into the visible world.

Matthew 11:12 says, *"And from the days of John the Baptist until now the kingdom of heaven suffereth violence, and the violent take it by force."* The original rendering of this verse says, "From the days of John the Baptist until now, the kingdom of Heaven has been administered by force and those in power control it."

Faith is a force that God has given to the citizens of the unseen world to superimpose their world upon the seen world and make the time zones of this earth work for them. Time works for us and can be subdued, once we understand faith. When we do not understand faith, it works against us. This forces us to conform to the dictates of this fallen world. But we are not of this world. We are of the Kingdom of God, and the kingdom of light. Those who are born again are born from above. This allows these new creations to be immune to the effects of the system of this world. We must use eternal laws to enforce the outcome of our circumstances. Through the law of faith, we have been divinely empowered with an ability to supersede the law of time. This is an attribute we receive from the inherent DNA of God in us.

We can easily understand faith, when we see how time is no longer the dominant factor in the equation standing between our desire and His purpose. Faith takes us up above the restrictive limitations of time. It enables us to speed things up and bring them into the now. What time declares a situation to be is no longer an issue. Time, having no power, must release that which is unseen and bow to faith, which is the greater force.

Faith is nothing more than reaching backward and forward, in the dimension of time. We actually have the power to manipulate time to suit ourselves and bring it into our present. While time declares that scheduled events were our past, realities appear locked away from our present existence and cannot be accessed, faith releases it into our now.

Because faith does not comprehend the confines and limitations of time, it is able to reach back into the past, forward (or upwards) into the future, all at the same time, and bring them all into the present. Therefore, faith is the past, present and future all wrapped up together in the now. Until we fully grasp the fact that faith always breaks the laws of time, we will always work our faith through time.

If we work it through time, we filter our faith through the natural instead of through the supernatural and rob ourselves of our divine rights.

"Now faith is the substance of things hoped for, the evidence of things not seen." (Hebrews 11:1)

God has created everything seen and unseen. He placed the substance of the visible, and the invisible world into the believer. What is inside of us holds both worlds together. Jesus walked in and out of the realm of eternity while in His earthly body. He defied the laws of time and mocked the dominion time had over man. Through this, He showed us how fragile time actually is.

The Syrophoenician woman was a Greek, excluded from the Covenants of Promise, and therefore did not qualify for the healing virtue of Jesus to touch her daughter. Jesus knew it wasn't their time. He was yet to die on the cross, so the Gentile nations had no access to His redemptive power.

So, if Jesus didn't heal by virtue of the Cross of Calvary, by what law did he do it? Was it mercy? No! There was another law operating; Jesus broke the laws of time that constrained them. He went back in time, to the foundation of the world, where the Lamb was slain before time ever was.

Just as an exploding star takes 300 years before the earth ever finds out about it, so Jesus was crucified, buried and raised before He ever got to the earth! When He came here, He was already dead. He was already raised. We saw Him after the fact! This is why when He was on the earth He traveled backward and forward in time, messing up their theology, and confusing the devil so that Lucifer was not certain whether Jesus was coming or going. There is nothing that can take place here upon the earth that hasn't already taken place in the Heavenlies. He could come to earth and act out His prophetic drama upon the earth because He had already died in the Heavenlies. He came to set the drama into time, to redeem man and the earth.

Romans 12:2 says, *"And be not conformed to this world: but be ye transformed by the renewing of your mind..."*

The idea conveyed here is that we are to renew our minds, suggesting that it once possessed certain knowledge, but something was lost and must be regained.

When the Apostle Paul says, "be not conformed to this world", he is saying do not be subdued to this world age, to time zones, or to the prison of time's limitations here upon this earth. If we are born again, our citizenship is in Heaven; however, our members are here upon the earth, we actually live in two places at the same time!

We are to think like Ambassadors from another planet, never forgetting that we are not subject to the dictates of this time realm— we have access to eternity by virtue of our Heavenly birthright.

Throughout his writings, Paul urged people to renew their minds, or to fine tune their mindset to the frequency of Heaven, in order to harmonize with the song of Heaven, or revelations coming forth fresh from the throne room of God.

CHAPTER ELEVEN

The Renewed Mind

The Lord has been so gracious to allow me so many revelations. I can barely open the pages of the Word of God without receiving some level of fresh revelatory insight.

The Bride must learn that there are two types of hearing. The first type of hearing involves the spirit part of man. The other is where the soul is involved. While revelation is first received in the spirit, it will work its way through the soul, then into the fleshy part of man.

I am going to make a statement here which you will have to read aloud so that the hearing of it will activate the revelation of it. There are things that were inside your spirit before you were given your earth consciousness. Did you say that out loud? If not, do it now!

The body is not the real you. We are spirit beings. We respond to those things in the spirit realm. When revelation is spoken the spirit part of us is activated. It is at that time that the revelation becomes matter in us. If you are a preacher, you will often find yourself preaching and something is dropped into your spirit. You will preach it right then and there, and as you speak it there is more light on that subject, even though you had not planned on speaking on that subject in your notes!

Maybe you have just been a good friend listening to one of your brothers, or sisters, as they pour their heart out to you about a crises in their life. As you listen to them, a thought comes into your mind which gives you some level of clarity as to the problem. As you venture into the discussion about their problem more and more light comes to rest on the issue. You are suddenly aware that what you have experienced is a revelatory event. Your spirit man heard something that your physical man could not hear.

You may be asking how is this possible? Let me explain it to you in this manner. You were birthed from eternity into time. You are not some afterthought of God. You are a product of His handiwork. By His own hand and voice He fashioned you after Himself. The Word of God speaks of those who He had foreknowledge of, He predestined them to become the sons of God. That entire passage shouts of premeditation, preplanning, research and development! He did not just get up one day and decided to create someone who looks like you, talks like you, acts like you, and is you. Before the foundation of the earth was even laid out, He had created you in Him! Can you get that into your spirit? You were in Him! He actually called you out of Himself into time. If you can accept that He is all that Heaven was, is and is to come, then you will suddenly see that you come from a world much different from this one.

I can hear those who are skeptical asking about those who are not serving the Lord. You want to know about them? They came from the same designed plan as you did. When God created mankind, He placed in them a mind, will and emotions. He also gave them the ability to choose. He gave man the right to make decisions, right or wrong. So, when you see the people not serving Him, you are actually seeing disobedient creations making the wrong choices.

As you read this book, you will find that every time you open the pages of the Bible you will receive revelation knowledge. Through pastoring, I learned that there are two types of hearing. One type of hearing is with your spirit, while another form of hearing is with your soul. Revelation must be received with your spirit. There are things that were inside your spirit before you were given earth consciousness. The body is not the real you. You were birthed from eternity into time. You are beginning to understand the world from which you came. Heaven is real.

These are the days of not just getting a touch but hearing what the Spirit is saying.

"I beseech you therefore, brethren, by the mercies of God, that ye present your bodies a living sacrifice, holy, acceptable unto God, which is your reasonable service. And be not conformed to this world: but be ye transformed by the renewing of your mind, that ye may prove what is that good, and acceptable, and perfect, will of God. For I say, through the grace given unto me, to every man that is among you, not to think of himself more

highly than he ought to think; but to think soberly, according as God hath dealt to every man the measure of faith. (Romans 12:1-3)

Say, "Be not conformed to this world." Say it again.

When you say it, say it with the absolute knowledge of what you are saying. It means that this world is in its right perspective in your life. It cannot exceed and override the realm of the Spirit. Your sense of reason has nothing to do with that world. That world is bigger than your ability to reason or understand it. Now say it again. "Be not conformed to this world."

There are missing time zones that are not recorded. There are things that happened in the realm of the Spirit that have not been recorded. They have not been written. That is the reason that people who are heavily Logos-minded could miss the river of God.

****

"Be not conformed to this world."

****

Because the river is not based on logos (the written word); it is based on Rhema (the spoken word). In the river you will have the common flow of God. Revelation knowledge will become the norm. So there are missing time zones. There are gaps on the earth. Not all of the things that God said and did are written. That is why in this age we must know the voice of the Spirit. We have to come to the place that we know what we hear we do not take for granted. That word which God is speaking to you (Rhema) is as much real as the written (Logos) and will never contradict it. The Glory of God came in the meeting in a church where I was ministering, and I saw missing times collide. When the times collided, I saw manifestations of the past that were not recorded.

There are things that Jesus did that are not even written.

"And there are also many other things which Jesus did, the which, if they should be written every one, I suppose that even the world itself could not contain the books that should be written." (John 21:25)

Jesus Christ did great and marvelous things. What then are the "greater works?" The greater works are in the new, but subconsciously we are still looking for characteristics of the old. There are manifestations of the Heavens, the realm of the Spirit that once visited the earth that men could not write about. Not all about Heaven is written.

I have been to Heaven quite a few times and I can tell you that everything is not written. There are things in the Heavens we have not yet conceived. Heaven is real. Heaven is still being unfolded.

There are things we do not understand. But we are going to understand them if we keep an open spirit. There are things that God is going to do now that our forefathers only had a foretaste of. The best is yet to come! That is the reason why there has been no time like our time. Why? The Bible says that in the end times God will compress time. (Rev 10:6) You have heard the expression, "Your whole life flashes before you."

So, if you are seventy-three years old, that many years will flash before you in a second. Some of you think you are old. You are not old if your whole life can flash before you in a second. God gave me this statement.

"The Bible says be not conformed to this world. The renewing of your mind is dispensational."

The word dispensational means a revealed period of time. I am going to use a natural truth to explain it. It is documented that man uses less than ten percent of his brain and thinks predominately on one side of his brain.

When man fell in the Garden, he lost use of the other side. The other side was akin to the Spirit realm. So when your mind is renewed you are taking back territories of the mind that the brain knew before. The mind was able to conceive and perceive the realm of the Spirit to such a degree that when Adam was walking physically here on the earth, he would be in the Heavens at the same time. Adam knew the seen and the unseen. He had no knowledge of limitation. He walked with God as God's equal.

CHAPTER TWELVE

Religion Conforms to Earth

A religious person does not believe in the renewal of the mind. A religious mind is conformed to the earth. That is how I can tell you what the Garden was like. Do you know what caused Adam to sin? When man was no longer being transformed, he conformed. We have this idea that Adam had only one transformation.

There are many transformations of the Spirit. There are dimensions of the Glory that we know nothing about. We will never exhaust the Glory of God. That is why it disturbs me when I hear pastors say, "We've seen it before." Well, if you have seen it all, you might as well go home to be with the Lord.

Adam traded the mind of God for common sense. Are you aware that your intellect by experience and function causes you to conform to time and matter? Because your mind conforms to time and matter, your intellect cannot understand anything that supersedes matter. Do you have any idea in the realm of the Spirit when Adam fell? Do you have any idea what Adam fell from? I don't think any of us do.

I do know Adam had the mind of God in the Garden of Eden. And through the fall, he traded the mind of God for common sense and intellectualism. This is why, in the Garden, Adam didn't need faith. We don't need faith when we have everything provided for us. God comes down and communes with you in the cool of the evening. That doesn't take faith.

Do you know when faith is required? It is when nothing is happening that we need faith to push our way into the Heavens. But when the Heavens are open it is another story. When Adam was ejected from the Garden, God had to give mankind faith. The first manifestation God gave man was faith because Adam needed faith to see back into the world that he just fell from.

I was at a meeting in Maine, and they brought a mentally retarded brother. As soon as I looked at him, I knew what to do. (God even showed me how to deal with Alzheimer's.) Don't reason. Just do it! As soon as I looked at him, I knew what to do. God told me, "Hold his hand and just run with him." I held his hand and as we started to run, his mind came back. The Lord spoke into my spirit,

"You speak first and then you think afterwards. The reverse is just as true. As you act, your thinking will catch up. Tell him to run."

First the man started to wiggle. Then he ran and we watched his mind come back. He had lost his mind through the use of drugs. Don't question it. Just do it. The realm of the Spirit is real. I saw the Throne of the God and the waters of God. Then, I saw fire come from the Throne and enter the water. I watched the water take on different characteristics. There are things that are coming forth in the river that you're not expecting.

We cannot do the same old things as before. When the fire of God begins to come into the river, we have to literally maintain an open spirit. If we come to the river with an agenda, it won't work. If we get in the River of God and keep our spirits open, we will be able to articulate the moving of God.

We will know the shifting, the timing and the moving of the Spirit. I understood in an instant what to do. If I had questioned, I would have lost it. There are things in the Spirit we can miss if we hesitate. Just do it! When we obey, God will start to show them to you.

One of the shortest Scriptures in the Bible is found in the Old Testament.

"And Enoch walked with God: and he was not; for God took him." (Genesis 5:24)

Why is there a mystery according to the walk? Walking is a principle of seeing. Some years ago, I had an accident and my back was damaged. The therapist told me that the nerve to your eyes is in your hands and feet. This explains that in the Spirit, at times, we only see when we touch someone. As Enoch was walking, he was seeing, and God took him.

There are things in the Spirit that we grow into. But there are things in the Spirit that we step into. Some think that there is a period of time to grow into the things we hear and see. When we step in, we will know it is happening now. The Lord told me, "Prayer demands a transcendence of self."

There is no warfare in the Glory. God is not at war with Himself. The warfare is to get into the Glory. If we pitch tent in our gifting, we will wear out, but we will never burn out if we live in His presence. We never will. Why? In the realm of the Glory our body clock does not work. We do not know time in His presence. We can be in a meeting that lasts five hours, but it only felt like an hour.

****

"There is no warfare in the Glory."

****

That is how we know when you have transcended. I am feeling a fire when I write this sentence. Is Satan defeated? Is he deformed and disarmed? Then why are you sick? Don't let the enemy twist what I am saying. Your prayer life is going to radically change. If Jesus did defeat Satan, if he is defeated in the realm of the Spirit, then is he now not defeated? In your soul that is part of self-maintenance. It is not someone else laying hands on you. Your personal walk with God is self-maintenance.

To come into this NEW walk we must transcend SELF. You can't cast out self; you must crucify it.

"And they that are Christ's have crucified the flesh with the affections and lusts." (Galatians 5:24)

If you crucify self, you might find out that you crucify cancer at the same time. Most of us subconsciously live a soulish life. Sickness and disease are real in a soulish life.

Your circumstances are real when you live in the realm of the soul. When you have really transcended your body and entered into His presence do you think you can dry up and burn out? Do you think you can be sick? No! Never!

When I was younger, I would go lay hands on folks as soon as the anointing fell.

And the Lord said, "Renny, listen and learn. Now don't just use your faith to do miracles. The greatest warfare today is in using your faith to take people to the place of My presence. That is the place of warfare, because everyone does not want to go. In the realm of the Spirit it does not take long to get there."

Each time we meet it should take less time to enter into His presence.

John said, *"And immediately I was in the spirit: and, behold, a throne was set in heaven, and one sat on the throne."* (Revelation 4:2)

In Ohio, there were tremendous signs and wonders in the meetings. One night the worship leader was caught up in the Spirit of God for hours. After the meeting I returned home to Texas. A few weeks later the pastor of the church called, "Sit down, I want to tell you something." He told me that the worship leader's nephew had died and she went immediately to the hospital.

When she saw the dead body, she said, "Lord, I am asking you to manifest the same Glory that you recently imparted to me. Send that same Glory into this hospital ward." Suddenly the cloud came in and the manifested presence of God came in the room. When it appeared, he came back to life. Hallelujah! It is documented. If we can stop feeling sorry for ourselves and get into His presence, God can move.

In old Pentecost we said, "Only believe." Today I just say, "Get into His presence." When you get there, you will find Him waiting. In His presence you will find everything you are ever going to need. Faith's fulfillment is entering into His presence. Man was ejected from that presence.

God wants us to get into His presence in a new way. It should not take us hours to get there. That is why we have so many miracles in our meetings. We preach that it doesn't take that long to get there. The secret of it is that you can't come before His face with your yokes still hanging on you. The yokes were broken at Calvary.

When a miracle realm comes in a meeting you must learn to take whatever you need. As soon as you sense that realm, stop right there and declare it. If you don't, it may never come again. That is why our spirits can enter in but our bodies can miss the benefits.

God wants you to come to a new place where it doesn't take you that long to get in His presence. One of the reasons we sing choruses is to build a new atmosphere. Some people cannot enter in unless they were there when the realm was built. The wisdom of the Spirit is that you have to build a realm. You cannot presume what God is going to do. Everyone may not be at the same place.

Even in taking the Lord's Supper the Bible says that we are to wait on each other. That means around His table, we do not all enter His presence at the same time. There are some who are forerunners, and they enter quickly. I just try to live there. That is how you get revelation knowledge—you just live there.

A blind girl was at one meeting and some folks were offended that I did not lay hands on her. We have got to get past the hand of the man and get into the presence of God for ourselves. This little blind girl was worshipping the Lord and suddenly both of her eyes popped open. There were many miracles that night, but I want to major on this one. I told the parents, "You know what struck me about your daughter? She entered the presence for herself."

Years ago, when I came back from the mission field and started preaching in the church, it was bewildering to see that nothing was happening. I wondered why and questioned the Lord, "Why isn't anything happening in the church today?"

He answered, *"The reason you see these things happening wherever you go is because you are walking in the governments, I have given you. That is why you can receive those things whether the church has it or not. You have to bring it to the church."*

What remains in a church is based on the foundation that has been laid. You have to minister where that church is. What has taken man years to build can be quickly destroyed. This is wisdom's secret. You cannot go in and bulldoze the pastor. When you do warfare in the realm of the Spirit and the ground is broken, then you will find he is open to change.

Can we bring what we receive from the Throne Room back to earth? The warfare happens when you are earth conscious. We receive in the Heavens, but warfare is to bring what you receive in the Heavens back to earth. Warfare is going to change. When you enter His presence, you don't need to war because in His presence, you rest. If you are still working, then you didn't enter into the rest. You don't struggle, because you have knowledge that you received from the Holy Spirit. In the Spirit things happen quickly. Eyeballs materialize instantly. Missing body parts manifest quickly.

God is calling some of us out of that which is good and taking us into that which is perfect. Some ministries are changing. The strength of our character is going to cause us to stand in that new place. Joyce Meyers has been known for saying, "New level, and a new devil."

****

"Unless God strengthens you, you can't stand in the new."

****

Unless God strengthens you, you can't stand in the new. That is why some of you should be on the platforms of the world, but the principalities of the world knocked you off. You must develop that inner strength to stand. There are some who have been in sin and have not seen the increase that is due.

The Lord said, *"You will never see the increase from where you are now. You will never see it in the realm of acceptable or even good. If you stay in one place too long your past comes back at the door."*

In reality, if you are not going forward, you are going backward, because in the realm of the Spirit there is no time. Past is only a name, but it knocks at your door, and instead of seeing the increase you see the decrease.

God is calling you out from what is good or acceptable because He wants you to walk in that which is "perfect."

"And be not conformed to this world: but be ye transformed by the renewing of your mind, that ye may prove what is that good, and acceptable, and perfect, will of God." (Romans 12:2)

Some of you are in that place right now. You have been faithful, and perhaps comfortable in the place of "acceptable." It was for a time period. But God is saying, "Come up higher." Until you do, you will never know the "perfect."

I have been to Heaven in the Spirit several times. Once when I went into the Throne Room it was as if the throne had divided into two separate pieces. I could see Jesus, but I could not see God, the Father. When a man is in the realm of the Spirit, communication is not with speech. Your questions are answered in His nonverbalized thoughts. When you are thinking, it often seems like a dream. Before you think it, it is known. No place terrified me as much as the Throne Room. I understand why many people never make it to this room.

In the outer court is where we all meet but it is time for you to have an audience with the King. We know the courtyards but when you know the Throne, you are different. Your ability to perceive and conceive is changed.

Because you are out of the body in the realm of the Spirit, there is nothing you can't see as you stand before His Throne. I could see the Holy Spirit. I could see Jesus. The Father's face was not seen. It may be difficult for some of you to comprehend that it is possible to enter His realm upon invitation. He commands us to enter into Him. As we do, we enter into another dimension which is not ruled by the dynamics of time. It is simply put—Now.

I have seen the times and seasons as God has laid them out for all mankind. While I have witnessed these times and seasons and they say, "This is the time period for this, or this is the time period for that." I have seen the great library in the Heavens. There are books regarding signs and wonders that have never been opened, while there are many which are even now being opened. As in all things in the ownership of God, there were more than man could count.

I truly think one of the more wonderful revelations for the believer about the Library of Heaven is that there is a book which has your name on it, as well as one with my name on it. It holds the destiny God has laid out for each one of us before the foundation of the earth was laid. Unlocking this book requires our will. We must accept the destiny written inside the book. To ignore, or show disregard for the written plan of God for us is to keep the book closed on the blessing He has in store for each one of us. He wants to give to you this book. Are you willing to receive it? Will you break through the mental blocks and receive your renewed mind? The Word will change you forever. Be not conformed. Be transformed.

Right now, pray this prayer aloud to the Lord, and watch the weight of heaviness lift from you.

"Father, in the name of Jesus I ask you to cleanse my mind by the washing of the water of the Word. Cleanse me from idle thoughts and open my mind to receive the perfect will of God. Prepare my heart and mind so that I might enter into the perfected plan you have for my life. Let me walk in your ways and think your thoughts. For Christ's sake I pray. Amen."

Renny McLean

CHAPTER THIRTEEN

Breakthrough

It is crucial in this hour that we hear the crystal-clear Word of God and let Him write on the tablets of our heart. If He writes the Word, it takes root deep in our spirit man and begins to grow. No one can wipe that tablet clean because God has written it and there should be only one response, "Amen Lord, so be it."

It is then that our spirit can be programmed to respond to what He is saying. We then have the capacity to open our spirits to new truth and revelation. When this occurs, we will experience a breakthrough into new realms of understanding God, His Word and His Purpose for us.

Many of us hear much discussion regarding breakthrough. So, what is a breakthrough? How do we recognize it? And of course, when do you know when the breakthrough has come and gone?

Here's an example of a breakthrough. After I was ministering one evening an individual walked up to me and asked, "Brother Renny, don't you think your preaching is a little extreme?" I responded, "No. The problem with most churches is that they have pitched their tent in the valley of repetition and refuse to be open to anything new." And let me explain to you why I sense that so strong in my spirit. We have come to be at home with the religious scheme of things. We are not seeking time with the Lord, we are timing the seeking of the Lord.

I crave the truth, no matter what the cost, and because of my love for truth, I have a major problem with religion. I've seen the destructive power, and the evil of tradition. When people pitch their tent in what they know, then they stop growing and stagnate in religion, tradition and self.

Once we have begun the renewal of our minds we then begin to move beyond our soulish intellect and make ourselves ready for a breakthrough into the new, or what I prefer to call the now. A breakthrough is a sudden burst of advanced knowledge that takes you past a point of defense. When people are not growing in knowledge and truth, they stay where they are. As some have stated with great contentment, "I am saved, sanctified and sitting, waiting on the Lord". That type of existence only denies the need to change and eliminates the opportunity for any level of breakthrough.

Until we get a breakthrough, we remain tied to the very things that God is trying to loose us from. When you get a sudden burst of revelation and realize that it's not coming from the hand of man, but from God, breakthrough has potential. When God cuts the cords of bondage, no man can stitch it back together. When you seek a breakthrough, are you prepared for the change? Do you really mean that you are a candidate for a breakthrough? If so, get ready, get ready!

God spoke this to me, "The things that are now coming forth on the earth from the eternal realm will remain unshaken. Only that which is eternal will remain."

Please note that He was speaking of those things coming from the eternal realm, not that which is in, of, or on the earth. This means many who are still relying on the old system of religion will be in for a shakedown. Man is faltering more and more, day by day. In the Body of Christ, we have to wade through far too much religion that it isn't surprising that the average believer doesn't know how to enter and stay in the presence of God.

The spirit of religion hates it when anyone is set free. The greatest wars on earth have been caused by religion. If you study the early years of European history, it will be filled with crusades in the name of the Church. The real truth is that they were not going to war in God's name, it was on behalf of the organized religious group in power at that time. If God elevates someone in our midst who doesn't do things the way we do them, we say that the move is not of God.

Instead of the church being productive in creating disciples, we are being counterproductive. We are losing those who once had a passionate desire for Christ. Instead of the church sensing the power of God, it is more attune to the power of the man, or woman, in the pulpit. The Gospel is being ignored. But it will not be allowed to be ignored for long. God is stirring up a company of believers who will not accept the status quo. A new day is birthing a resurrection of love and devotion to the King of Kings, and Lord of Lords.

Present things are being disturbed by the eternal. God is pushing out that which is convenient and temporal in order to establish that which is permanent.

Allow me to make an observation if you will. In the West, most of you haven't seen anything yet. God is bringing breakthroughs from all varieties of religious spirits wherever the leaders allow Him to move. We have to expect God to show up mightily in the days to come. He is doing new things right now.

****

"You have soul ties."

****

Some of you are not free to walk in God's calling for your life. Do you know why some of you have not experienced a clean-cut breakthrough? You have soul ties. Soul ties are bonds with family, associates, and other relationships. You know you have a soul tie when God has spoken to you, but the people to whom you're tied take priority in your life. Then God takes second place. Is it any wonder you can come to a meeting, get pumped up, stirred up, and then go back to the same soulish relationships? The cord wasn't cut from your soul ties.

Here's a good example: If you cannot find life in the root, then the tree cannot bear fruit. The only way a tree can bear fruit is if life is also in its root. We are looking at the tree as it appears above ground, but its real potential is in its roots. You must get to the root cause of your bondage. Some of you need to cut the soulish ties of intimidation and fear of man's sanctioning, otherwise you will never get your breakthrough.

Your mind is faithful to what you know and when something new comes along you reject it. No matter how alive you think you are, if you haven't severed all ties to the former, you will not flow in the new. God's mercies are new every morning.

Some of you have never had that breakthrough because your ties were never fully cut. You feel guilty and end up saying, "I made a mistake." If you understand destiny, it could never have been a mistake. It was a mistake in your eyes only because you couldn't see the end from the beginning and became discouraged. People manipulated you to come back.

When your grace level falls, you can't tolerate their errors anymore. Then you will know God has cut the cords and given you a breakthrough. It doesn't necessarily mean that God is trying to remove that person out of your life completely, He's merely changing the basis of that relationship. If you don't allow Him to change you, those soul ties will sneak in to drag you back to where you started, and your breakthrough will not be sustained.

Luke 12:34 says, *"For where your treasure is, there will your heart be also."*

The Hebrew version actually says: "Where a man's heart is, there he is." You are spirit, soul and body. Your body is your earth suit but your spirit travels constantly. Yet, you have conformed to matter, which is visible. If matter is the basis of your reality, you need a breakthrough from matter.

Prophecy is the means by which time is created. Revelation is the means by which that time is made known. When revelation is made known, can it possibly be in another time? Some people presume that when the man of God touches them everything will be all right. God is a spirit. That means He lives in you. He is as near to you as He is to me. The same anointing that is on me is in you but you have put matter between that. You have set the time of your miracle by limiting it to time and space. You have said when he touches you such and such will happen. Too many prophets today are putting into the future what God has already done and is available now.

The church speaks of revival. I can't call it revival when a dead person comes to life and a blind one sees. I've witnessed that for the last twenty-five years. I met the Lord when I was five years old and received my call at the age of seven. When I was nine, God used me to cast out devils. He was using me to heal the sick when I was ten and to raise the dead at fourteen years of age.

I had a breakthrough when I was a young boy. I learned that God is not way out there somewhere. He is inside of me. The One inside of me is the same yesterday, today and forever.

"Jesus Christ the same yesterday, and today, and forever." (Hebrews 13:8)

I am not waiting for a move of God. It is within me. Wherever I go, the devil has to leave because of the presence and power of Christ in me. There are no options; Jesus knew His authority.

The Bible tells us "They killed Jesus not because He was a prophet but because He said He was the Son of God." They accepted Him in the fivefold ministry according to Ephesians 4. They accepted Him as a teacher but they had problems when He said He was the Son of God. By that declaration He was saying He was equal with God. The Bible says you are a Son of God.

"Beloved, now are we the sons of God, and it doth not yet appear what we shall be: but we know that, when he shall appear, we shall be like him; for we shall see him as he is." (1 John 3:2)

The revelation is in using the words joint heir—to be made equal with. (Romans. 8:17) In equality priority goes to the one who was first. In Romans it says Christ has the full preeminence. We are his brethren, but He was the first. We are made equal to Him. When the devil looks at you he sees God in flesh, in human form. He doesn't hang around that.

When I was a young man conducting and attended conferences and crusades all over England, the devils stopped coming. The devil knows who can pray. Many walk in the knowledge of ignorance. Satan cannot get advantage over us unless we are ignorant of his devices.

"Lest Satan should get an advantage of us: for we are not ignorant of his devices." (2 Cor 2:11)

Jesus had a breakthrough over matter.

When He went to raise Lazarus from the dead, the disciples told Him that the Jews were seeking to stone Him.

"His disciples say unto him, Master, the Jews of late sought to stone thee; and goest thou thither again? Jesus answered, Are there not twelve hours in the day? If any man walk in the day, he stumbleth not, because he seeth the light of this world. But if a man walk in the night, he stumbleth, because there is no light in him." (John 11:8-10)

When God calls someone, the first thing He imparts is a breakthrough—a sudden burst of advanced knowledge. There are signs telling whether a person has changed or not. We know when there is no change in a person when they wreak havoc out of something you give them to do. They did not have the grace for it and the signs were there. If a person is changed, then there is the grace for the job. They flow with the Spirit.

I'm tired of the devil taking the church for a ride because we do not see the obvious. Wake up and declare truth. Truth isn't popular but truth will remain. Truth is an absolute. You don't negotiate with an absolute. The Truth causes a thing to be. What you see and feel is of no consequence. If you are wrong, you're wrong. If you are right, you're right. God's Word is right.

"Heaven and earth shall pass away, but my words shall not pass away." (Matthew 24:35)

Do you think God is going to change His mind about His Word? What He said about character years ago still stands. It's still a requirement today. What are the strongholds of your life and environment? What makes you act the way you do? What is pulling something out of you that you don't understand?

There's a law regarding your environment. When you separate a fish from water, it dies. Life corresponds to environment. When you pull a tree from the ground, it dies. When you separate someone from a religious environment, their religion dies. When God separates you from something, the ties are severed. If you go back into that environment, nothing can pull you anymore. You're in the environment, but you're totally free and delivered. The principle is that God's life flows when you are rid of hindering forces. When opposition faces hinderance in the Glory it will retreat.

Sometimes there are situations where you should not return to your environment. I was counseling a brother who said, "I have AIDS and I believe God will set me free from it." (We have seen hundreds set free from AIDS.) I said, "Okay, but when you're delivered, don't go back to the place where you acquired the condition." If the lifestyle doesn't change, you will go back to what you were. AIDS was not the problem. AIDS was the symptom. His environment was the problem.

Jesus made this statement, *"For the prince of this world cometh, and hath nothing in me."* John 14:30 (KJV)

Satan couldn't accuse Jesus of lying, stealing, or immorality. Why? It is because those things were never in Jesus.

****

"Time is matter that is dissolving."

****

This revelation must come before there is a breakthrough. Some pastors have a problem in leading people to a breakthrough because they have never had one for themselves. They are not free. You are free to have a breakthrough when you separate from illegal environments. Once free, they will be able to help others. The meaning of the word stronghold is the basis from which something functions. It is a thought or ideology which is fiercely defended. Did Jesus defeat Satan? The Bible says that He destroyed, disarmed and dethroned him. Did Jesus destroy the power of sickness, disease and death at the cross? The Bible says in Ephesians 2:15 that He abolished it. When strongholds are broken then breakthroughs will come. Whom the Son sets free is free indeed (John 8:36).

Time is matter that is dissolving. Our environment has caused us to conform to matter. Now we know why we need a breakthrough from our environment. Until you break through from what appears to be real to you, the curse is still visible to you. How can the curse be real to you if it was broken at the cross? The new redeemed creature knows the difference. The new creature knows how to go beyond to where they can obtain mercy. The new creature does not walk by sight, but by faith! The devil is dethroned, disarmed, destroyed and defeated. If he is all these things, then how can he do what he does to us? We let him. Every time we do what we ought not to do, it becomes a replay of what Adam did. This is the importance of a breakthrough from your environment. We are victims of our own environments because we are the product of our environment. Until you have a breakthrough from your environment, you are a victim of lower matter. Satan has a plan and purpose for everyone. There are no exceptions.

Satan's plan comes under two words: environmental control. His plan is facilitated through environmental control, which explains why you are the way you are. It is important for you to know who you are. You are the product of your environment. You may have left Egypt, but this does not mean Egypt has left you.

Moses had a breakthrough. When God called Moses back to Egypt, he gave him a breakthrough from his environment. At the burning bush God told Moses to take off his sandals and leave his environment of forty years of desert. He had entered into the environmental realm of God. Moses had another breakthrough with a friend in Egypt. Moses was raised in the palace of the Pharaoh. We have a distorted image of Moses. He was a man just like any Egyptian until he met God. He did not know God because he wasn't raised as a Hebrew. He was raised as an Egyptian. It was normal in that day for the sons of Pharaoh to know witchcraft. They were entertained by it and they believed in it. They worshiped their crocodile gods, the sun, moon and the stars. Moses was a believer in all of these idols. But God called him aside and he had a divine encounter with his God. He had a breakthrough from his old environment. Egypt no longer meant anything or had any power over Moses.

There is a Scripture in the Bible that says, *"Whatsoever ye shall bind on earth shall be bound in heaven: and whatsoever ye shall loose on earth shall be loosed in heaven."* (Matthew 18:18)

I want you to picture Moses going back to Pharaoh. If I were to ask you what was the strongest miracle that ever took place in Egypt, you would probably say, the parting of the Red Sea. It was awesome and powerful, but we learned a truth. They could not walk on the water, so God allowed them to walk on the earth under the water.

Moses and Aaron now come before Pharaoh. Moses throws down his rod. He knew what the wizards would do. He had seen it often. He threw down his rod and the wizards threw down their rods. What did the rods of the wizards turn to? Before their eyes the rods became snakes. Look at an Egyptian mummy, and you will see a king cobra, a snake. It represents the domain of that Pharaoh, his sphere of influence and his measure of rule. The snakes of Moses' rod swallowed snakes from the wizard's rods.

Jesus said you cannot enter a man's house unless you bind the strong man first.

> *"No man can enter into a strong man's house, and spoil his goods, except he will first bind the strong man; and then he will spoil his house."* (Mark 3:27)

Why could Moses walk in and out of Pharaoh's house and Pharaoh not touch him? Pharaoh was bound. This is why Moses could walk in and out as he pleased. What happened? Moses had a breakthrough from his environment. Some of you need a breakthrough from culture. When you get a breakthrough from your culture, you can preach, witness, and sing to anybody. When you get a breakthrough, you transcend yourself and circumstances. The issue is, are you willing to transcend? Do you want a breakthrough?

Faith affirms the invisible as reality. When you have a breakthrough from your environment, faith affirms the invisible as its reality. Faith does not affirm the seen. Faith transcends the seen because it knows the seen is temporal. Faith affirms reality. It supersedes reason. It supersedes your head and your intellectualism. It supersedes the counterfeit because the counterfeit knows it isn't real. Faith supersedes the seen. It supersedes the counterfeit knowledge that thinks it knows more than God. Faith supersedes it and steps on the counterfeit. It puts the counterfeit under its foot. It says you are not real. Give them a breakthrough, Lord!

Jesus is coming and our time is short. Either you want to be free, or you don't. You are either willing to change or you aren't. You are willing for a breakthrough, or you are not. What is it going to be?

God is redeeming the times. If you have been spat upon and abused, then God can make the devil pay for everything he stole from your life. How is God going to redeem the time for someone who has a case that has been in the courts for ten or fifteen years, especially if we don't have ten or fifteen years left?

Time is only relevant for those who primarily depend on earthly sources. In the Spirit time does not exist. So where do you think we are going for our answers? Don't lose sight of the fact that our time is about to break forth. This is our season and our hour. We are no longer going to be abused. We are going to walk in what God has purposed and put in our life.

You are going to come to the place where you realize the gates of hell cannot prevail against what God is doing in the earth. You never thought the day would get here but that day has come. This is the good news. It is not just today's front-page news; it is reality. You can break through and be free at last. Forget your human lifelines and forget what man says about you. Be like Paul who had learned to confer not with flesh and blood.

You have been denied your rights and had every reason to quit. In seeking God, you will find your place in Him. You will know God put you there. Jesus did not go through hell for you to sit on the sidelines and watch the parade go by. You have to know this came straight from the throne of God. The greater Glory is working in favor of your circumstances.

You are called. Living in His Glory is your destiny. Would you like me to tell you how He is going to redeem the times?

"And I will restore to you the years that the locust hath eaten, the cankerworm, and the caterpillar, and the palmerworm, my great army which I sent among you." (Joel 2:25)

He is going to take a year as a month. A month will be like a week. A week will be like a day. In six weeks, God can give you back what you lost in ten years.

God is doing something fresh and different in your spirit. You can feel the life of God surging through your being. What is God doing? He is lifting a remnant of people who dared to change and cross the line. Believe me, the best is yet to come. Now All the Jewish feasts are applicable to today's church. They are The Feast of Passover, The Feast of Pentecost and The Feast of Tabernacles. These feasts represent the three realms of the supernatural. Passover symbolizes faith. Pentecost symbolizes the anointing. Tabernacles symbolizes the Glory. The problem today is that we are trying to get people to have a Tabernacle when they haven't had a Pentecost. What does Passover mean? It symbolizes the faith realm. If Passover means faith, and faith means Passover, then it means to pass over—from the natural to the spiritual, from the seen to the unseen.

****

"Jesus brought the future into the 'now'."

****

When you have stepped over, the unseen becomes the seen. You have passed over and the seen is no longer your reality. When you pass over your means of determining reality is faith. Now you don't have to look with eyes of the flesh. You pass over. If we barely understand faith, how do we really understand what the anointing is all about? The Bible says that Jesus had the Spirit without measure. He had the anointing without measure. Faith is the structure of the invisible realm.

There is a Scripture in the Bible that says God declares *"...the end from the beginning and the beginning from the end,"* Isaiah 46:10 (NKJV).

You know what qualifies now as now? "Hope for." Hope for was converted into the evidence and evidence was converted into substance and when it was converted into the substance, it became now. You don't need to look to what you already have. We have been taught subconsciously to disassociate ourselves from faith. Now you understand why the verse starts out with the word, "now". What happened? Jesus brought the future into the "now".

Faith is seeing what you hoped for becoming reality. The Bible says Jesus is the author and the Finisher of our faith. Joel looked into another time that wasn't yet revealed. You will often see this word declare, not so much in the New Testament, as there was nothing left to declare. Jesus said, "It is finished." The purest definition of declare means to bring something forth. Do you know why the prophets had to bring something forth? Jesus hadn't died yet. Jesus' death brought something forth. He said, "It is finished." You don't need to bring something forth which already exists.

Faith's measure of rule is the unseen. What is faith's measure of rule? You will see in the New Testament, the word measure. The dictionary defines the word measure as an amount. It doesn't mean that in the original language. It means your sphere of influence and rule. The issue is: where is faith's measure of rule? Read the verse again.

"Now faith is the substance of things hoped for, the evidence of things not seen." (Hebrews 11:1)

Faith's measure of rule is not the matter you see. Faith's measure of rule is in the realm that supersedes the matter that you can see. It's another world. Faith's measure of rule is the unseen. The difficulty is nobody is seeing. We are just confessing. We are trying to call what we have not seen. We have mistaken faith for presumption. Jesus said, "I only say those things that I hear My Father say and what I see."

"Then answered Jesus and said unto them, Verily, verily, I say unto you, The Son can do nothing of himself, but what he seeth the Father do: for what things soever he doeth, these also doeth the Son likewise." (John 5:19)

If you divorce faith from grace, you have a doctrine of works. It is not how much faith you have. It is because of what He has already done. By grace are you saved, as the Word of God declares. How does this happen? It happens through faith, and not your faith in the first place. You couldn't do it if you tried. It is the gift of God, lest any man should boast.

"For by grace are ye saved through faith; and that not of yourselves: it is the gift of God." (Ephesians 2:8)

Do you know why God is going to do certain things for you? You are His child. You have His favor, and God does a lot of things by favor that you don't even deserve. It wasn't because you had faith to believe it. He did it because He wants you to see His nature at work for you.

You think it was because of what you believe. Number one, it was because of what He did. Secondly, it is because He simply said it. Where were you when He said "Let there be light?" He is perfectly capable of doing it. It wasn't because you had faith. It was because He said it.

My Bible says, *"God is not a man, that he should lie; neither the son of man, that he should repent: hath he said, and shall he not do it?"* (Numbers. 23:19)

Let's be real. There have been times when God has done something for you and you weren't even walking right. How can you claim it is because of your faith? It has nothing to do with your faith. It was because of grace. Do you know how many people have died physically because they were told they didn't have enough faith?

Do you believe that God is the supreme intelligence? Don't you think the God of the universe had enough sense to give you the faith you need? Either God is backward or stupid, which would neither testify to His omnipotence or His power. Or could it be that there are some things we have missed? Sadly, we have missed it. Are you aware that when you say you don't have enough faith, you are saying, that God in His all-wise counsel, didn't give you enough? I know people who are talked out of the little faith they have. That is part of the problem. You don't have any faith in what you really have. Faith's measure is the unseen.

Faith's measure of rule is not the seen, but the unseen. Faith opens to us the world, the realm, and the zone that was before time. Do you know why God gave you faith? Do you know why God gave man faith when He threw man out of the garden? Unless God gave man faith, man had no way of seeing back into the world He came from. So God gave man faith. Faith opens up the world before time. We are running out of time. Time is rubbing up against eternity. How is Joel's prophecy going to be fulfilled if we are running of time? He said in Joel 2:25, "I will restore the years to you that the cankerworm has eaten."

How is that going to happen if we are running out of time? I'll tell you how. A year is coming as a month. A month is coming as a week and a day is coming as an hour. Time is growing short because time is running into eternity.

****

"Time is growing short because time is running into eternity."

****

We are approaching an era where eternity will be named as the age. Time, as you once knew it, is not time, as you know it now. What is happening? Eternity is running into time. We are approaching the day that time was created. You will see it much clearer when we come back into the day in which man was created. God made man in the Garden of Eden. There is not a time on record that tells you how long Adam was in the Garden because eternity was the atmosphere of the earth. There were two realms. When man sinned, he was thrown outside the garden. This is when age began. When age began, Adam had so much of that realm still in him that he was able to live on the residue 936 years. The residue was that strong. We are in the day of the rest of God. Time is a form of matter that is dissolving even as I am talking to you. Are you aware that your circumstances are the product of time? Even as I am talking, your circumstances are dissolving. We look not at the things that are seen, but at the things that are unseen. The things that are unseen are eternal.

Time is a form of matter that is dissolving. Our environment has caused us to conform to matter. Now you know why we need a breakthrough from our environment. God has to give you a breakthrough from what you perceive is your reality. Until you get a breakthrough, the curse will have a preeminence in your life. How can the curse be a greater reality in your life if it was broken at the cross? The new creature knows differently. The new creature knows how to go beyond where they find mercy. The new creature walks by faith. The devil is dethroned, disarmed, destroyed and defeated. If he is all these things, then how can he do what he does to us? We let him. Every time we do what we are not supposed to do, it is nothing more than a replay of Adam's fall.

After you have a breakthrough from your environment, faith affirms the invisible as its reality. Faith transcends the seen, because it knows the seen is temporal. Faith affirms reality, superseding reason and intellectualism. Faith supersedes the seen and the counterfeit knowledge that exalts itself against the knowledge of God.

Faith affirms God as God and nothing else. Now you know why it says, *"For he that cometh to God must believe that he is,"* (Hebrews 11:6). Faith affirms God, a supernatural being having supernatural ability—who demands to be worshipped. When faith affirms God, God affirms things. Seek first His Kingdom. Affirm the Kingdom of God and all His righteousness and all these things will be added to you. The concern is that you affirm things. You often affirm a thing and don't know if it is the will of God. If you seek God first, then you would know. When you do know and the devil comes before you, it makes no difference. When it comes to infirmities such as diabetes or high blood pressure, it makes no difference. Lack or poverty make no difference. It doesn't matter because I know in whom I have believed. I am persuaded. When you know and are persuaded, the enemy cannot shake you.

"For the which cause I also suffer these things: nevertheless I am not ashamed: for I know whom I have believed, and am persuaded that he is able to keep that which I have committed unto him against that day." (2 Timothy 1:12)

Most of us affirm our situations and you know why God does not affirm them? They are out of order. You know what the order is...seek ye first.... When you seek Him first, does it really make any difference what the doctor tells you? Does it matter what your bank manager tells you? Absolutely not.

In transcending yourself, you surpass the temporal to touch the eternal. Each time you transcend you always lay hold of the eternal, because time can only go so far. When the mind is renewed, revelation elevates man above matter. Revelation elevates you above the present age. You understand that the eternal age dictates to the present age. You'll never fully understand the present age until you understand the eternal age. Revelation elevates you above matter. Faith comes first and then comes the revelation.

The Bible says:

"How by revelation, he made known unto me the mystery I wrote in a few words. Whereby, when you read, you may understand my knowledge. In the mystery of Christ, which in other ages was not known to the sons of man,

as it is now revealed unto His holy apostles and prophets by His Spirit. And to make all men see what is the fellowship of the mystery of the beginning of the world had been hid in God who created all things by Jesus Christ. To the intent that now, unto the principalities and powers in the Heavenly places might be known by the church the manifold wisdom of God according to the eternal purpose in Jesus our Lord. In whom we have boldness and access with confidence by faith with Him." (Ephesians 3:3-12)

Until the revelation comes, you have no access to the eternal. That is why we can't explain why there are some things that haven't happened yet unless God puts that faith in your spirit according to the revelation. Revelation precedes an impartation of faith. That is why faith comes by hearing the word of God. It's smooth sailing when the revelation comes and then faith abides. Your obstacle is in not having much revelation to give you access to the new things in the realm of the Spirit that God wants to do. The average person in the church does not want to hear anything new. They want to hear ABC kindergarten faith. Until it is made known, you don't have the faith to do the things you can do.

We've pretty much brought this thinking into the church. A well-known man of God did something he shouldn't have done. I said to him, "Sir, if God told you to do that, then He can supply. When the supply does not come, then God surely didn't say it." You can't hold God accountable for something He never said. If He said it, then He is accountable. If He said it, He is first of all accountable to Himself. Secondly, He is accountable to you. If God has told you that He is going to do something, then it makes no difference what Satan says. If God says it, then it will happen. It isn't how much faith you have. It's because He said it.

Revelation provides you access to the highest realm of substance: the invisible. The name of the matter we cannot see is the substance from which God formulates things. This is what He has put resident in you. It is a five-letter word called faith. Faith is not a confession; it is what you have. I'm talking about the God of the universe putting something supernatural inside of you that controls the three realms of matter. If you have revelation, you can deal with matter, but without it you cannot.

The Bible tells us what to say and how to say it. Do you know what that means? Jesus wasn't imitating the anointing of someone else. You don't want to go down that road. He wasn't trying to do what He saw some successful ministers do. He operated on His own faith. You cannot access, or function, on someone else's faith. It might work for them, because it is a Rhema word. If you get a Rhema (spoken word of God to your spirit) then you have no problem.

Twelve years ago, I went to Sierra Leone, Africa. I have traveled the Mediterranean, Israel, and the Middle East. I have preached to the masses and all kinds of people. I ministered to Kings and Queens and people who simply thought they were. As we were preparing to leave for Sierra Leone we went to Heathrow Airport in London, England. I had my passport and my ticket, but I did not have a visa (you do need a visa to get into Sierra Leone).

I went to the British Airway flight agent. "Good afternoon, madam," I said. She replied, "Do you have your visa, Sir?" I asked, "What for?" She said, "You need a visa to go." I told her, "I'm sorry, I did not know this." She said, "Rev. McLean, you cannot go." "I've got to go, I'm a preacher," I replied. "I'm sorry, Reverend McLean, you cannot go." "If I'm not going, that plane will not move." You cannot say it that unless you know it. My wife was next to me and she said, "Renny, you can't say that." I responded, "I am going on that plane. If God wants me on that plane, He will send me. That is if God really spoke" "Did God tell you?" Marina asked.

I stood there and eyeballed that lady and said, "That plane is not going anywhere unless I am on it." I sat down and raised my hands. "Renny you are definitely a man of faith," Marina answered. "Devil, I dare you to get the plane out of my hand," I declared. I held my hand up and I saw the plane in my hand. One hour passed and the plane could not move. Two hours passed and the plane couldn't move. Three hours passed and the plane did not move. Five hours passed and the plane did not move. They deplaned all of the passengers. They couldn't figure out what was wrong because everything appeared to be normal. Now, it's going on seven hours, and I am drinking tea and hot chocolate. I told Marina, "You can go home now. The plane is not going unless I am on it."

The lady came back after eating her lunch, saw me sitting there holding my hand up in the air and said, "How come you have got your hand like that?" I answered, "I am holding the plane." She looked at me with one of those "Boy, you're some kind of nut case" looks. Oh well, the church has looked the fool, because we didn't know whether we'd heard from God or not. I said, "Lady, I told you that plane is not going anywhere unless I am on it." She said, "I remember you saying that and you are still here." "Yes, and that plane will be down another seven hours if I am not on it," I responded.

She retorted, "If this is true about you and God, then you get on the plane and see if it will move." Can you just imagine the smirk on her face? I got on that plane and said, "In the name of Jesus, I release this plane." The flight attendants slammed the door shut. The plane proceeded to the main runway.

"Why weren't you on here before?" the people onboard asked me. I said, "Well, it was because of me the plane didn't move." (Not the best way to win friends and influence people.)

The problem with us today is that we have diluted what the Bible calls faith. We have turned faith into a cheap commodity. No wonder it does not work. Is the devil a liar? Yes. So, if the devil is a liar, then why should we believe him? I feel a breakthrough in the offering. Hope is dependent on faith for something to come to full fruition. The problem is that we live in two separate worlds. The Bible says that hope deferred makes the heart sick (Proverbs. 13:12). Now faith is!

In my own mind, I do not accept limits. I don't see four walls. Now faith is! If you are still seeing your circumstance, then you are not yet seeing in the spirit. Faith is the foundation of hope. Now faith is! How can hope be present if in your mind you are thinking in future tense? Deep calls unto deep. Hope calls unto evidence. Evidence calls unto substance. Substance calls unto now. Hope calls the beyond to the here and now. Hope calls unto faith for its reality. Hope is calling out for reality, coexistence, and actuality. Hope depends on faith for its structure, its embodiment. You must not stand on anything but faith in the now.

****

"Faith imposes eternity into time."

****

Faith imposes eternity into time. Time lines up with what God says you are and have now! It is not what time says. It is what God says. Faith stands on what has already been predetermined. That's why you have expectancy. That expectancy tells you something is about to happen. That's why you shout the praises of God. Something is about to happen. Because you know something is about to happen, you praise God in advance.

Act as if you know something is about to happen. I couldn't care less about what I see. Something is about to happen. Because you know something is about to happen, you sing, "I will enter into His gates with thanksgiving in my heart. I am going to enter His courts with thanksgiving." Act as if you know something is about to happen. Dance about it; shout about it. You know you are coming out of debt. You know you are coming out of sickness. You know you are coming out of disease. You know your unsaved loved ones are going to be saved. That is why you are shouting.

When you seek Him first, and you know who you are, do you think it makes any difference what the doctor tells you? Does it make any difference what the Bible says about what you are able to bear? Yes. God is saying, "You can't pass this point until you get your miracle. I am going to hold time here until I get my miracle." Time is not going to say to you, at this time, time will be no more. Eternity will step into time. Faith is a decision based on advanced knowledge. Faith stands and acts on what is predetermined.

The woman with the issue of blood didn't wait until she saw who was going to be at church. She saw it long before. "I want to go see this man. I am predetermined within myself. If I touch the hem of His garment, I will be whole." I imagine she was probably the weakest one in the crowd surrounding Jesus that day but purpose and focus made her press through. She took hold of her miracle. Faith is a decision based on advanced knowledge. Then it becomes an act of your will. The issue is, do you really want it? When you really want it, you are determined. It makes no difference when your mind is made up and you know what God has for you. When you believe, it is going to happen. In fact, it has already happened.

Faith breaks the law of time every time.

"The woman was a Greek, a Syrophenician by nation; and she besought him that he would cast forth the devil out of her daughter." (Mark 7:26)

Jesus didn't even speak to her. She looked at him. Free yourself of your religion. Finally, when He did speak, "It is not your time. I have not come to you." He just sat there. This woman said, "Even the dogs eat the crumbs from the master's table." Jesus said, "Woman, great is thy faith." He healed a Gentile before her time. How could he do that? In time the cross had not occurred yet. But the Lamb was slain before the foundations of time (Rev. 13:8). He just went into the foundations of the world where the stripes were already laid. Faith breaks the law of time every time.

Unbelief in God's Word provides alternatives for faith. Do you know what the problem is with the church? We have substituted alternatives for faith. You know why you use other alternatives? It's because you don't really believe. You're not really sure that God meant what He said. But when you are sure, you know the way it is supposed to be. Then you will say, "It's going to work in my favor. It makes no difference what it looks like. It makes no difference what people say."

The issue is when are you going to take it? The price was paid for your sickness. The price was paid for your property. The price was paid for your debt. When are you going to take it? When are you going to stop being double-minded about it? When are you going to stop making an alternative? What are you really going to believe?

Raise your hands right now, from where you are to where you're going. I want you to start giving Him praise. Give Him praise like a mighty river. I will enter His gates with thanksgiving in my heart. I will say, "This is the day the Lord has made and I will rejoice and be glad in it." Glory! NOW!

Peter went to the Mount of Transfiguration. This had always bothered me. I never understood how Jesus took Peter, James and John to the Mount of Transfiguration. You would think Jesus would want them to evangelize with what they had seen and experienced. Peter was caught up in the height of that Glory and then Jesus came out and said, "Tell no man" (Mark 9:9). Peter saw the realm, but he had not conceived the realm. The secret of it is, when you have conceived a realm, your voice carries that realm. Peter had not yet received that realm. That's why Jesus said unto him, "Don't say anything yet." When Peter received the Holy Ghost, he understood spiritual things, because he was no longer carnally minded. Make sure your spirit conceives a realm.

I like to participate in everything that goes on in a meeting whether it's hopping, skipping, running or whatever. You have to catch the realm. This is the day when you are not necessarily going to minister what you have studied. You have to catch the flow of the river to know the stream of God. Do not go ahead of it because you have head knowledge. Also, make sure the river is in the word you are speaking. Peter saw miracles; in fact all the disciples saw miracles. Seeing signs and wonders was not a problem for them, even when Jesus came to them walking on the water, which was no ordinary miracle.

We are not God. We are made in His image, after His likeness, but we are given the Glory in which God Himself operates. When you get into that realm, it bypasses your faith. It bypasses your calling, your office, your ministry, because it is a sovereign act of God. When Jesus was going to the home of Jarius, there were miracles on the way. Because number one, there was a woman with the issue of blood. When I come into a service, I have people all around me asking me questions much like they did the Son of God. I often wonder, if that happens to me, then what do you think it was like for Jesus?

Many people must have touched him. The disciples went so far as to say, "What's your problem? Everybody is touching you." But not everybody that's touching you is making a demand on your gift. When faith makes a demand, there is a withdrawal. Although others touched Him, that woman's touch was the only one that Jesus identified with. It pulled something into manifestation that Jesus was not even looking for. The Bible states that He was heading for the home of Jarius. Do you know at times what happens when a man of God is preaching? Thank God for the gifts of the Spirit. I've been walking in them since I was a child. However, if you know how to put a demand on the Word as it goes forth, you can receive from the Spirit, right there in your seat, as the minister speaks. The church, at large, misses the greatest manifestations of miracles because we're stuck in the laying of hands as the primary way to receive.

I heard Oral Roberts make this statement, "After laying my hands on so many people, I actually wore my shoulders out." In those days, they did not have the concept of the mass miracle. Everybody had the concept of the laying of hands. Unless people are trained and understand your flow when you are ministering, they will never get the fullness of the anointing that's on your life. Why? They are looking for it in a place that it's not coming from. That's the reason why when you pastor and minister to people on a continual basis, you must teach the people how to be a recipient of your anointing. They need to understand your flow. I have seen the dead raised, and thousands of lame walk. Often, the bigger the crowd, the bigger the miracle you will see. That's common sense. If you're preaching to fifty, you'll only see fifty, because that's all there is.

That's all the demand is for. A church stops growing when their expectation dwindles.

When I went to Mombassa, Kenya, about 15 years ago, a brother was there who was about as tall as me. (I'm 6'2".) This brother had one leg that was dangling at his side. Seeing him walk was not a problem for me. I had seen people walk miraculously but I'd never seen a man with a leg that short before. That afternoon in Mombassa, Kenya, I preached like a man from another world. I was caught up in the Word that was being preached. In fact, I was so caught up that God was saying that I didn't see the man that was standing before me. In the Spirit, when I looked back at him, his leg was short.

God said to me, *"This is how I see the leg, Renny. He's been sitting on his leg all his life. His leg is still there. He can't see it."*

God didn't say the leg wasn't there. He said that the man couldn't see it. While I was standing there preaching, the Lord flashed this scripture back into my spirit.

> *"But is now made manifest by the appearing of our Saviour Jesus Christ, who hath abolished death, and hath brought life and immortality to light through the gospel."* (2 Timothy 1:10)

The Lord told me, *"You don't pray up the power, you preach the power."*

I haven't read books about that, nor had any formula. I hadn't seen anybody I knew deal with a miracle like this one. I didn't know what to do.

The Lord said to me, *"Stand there. Preach until you see it."*

It makes you wonder what preaching is when nothing is happening because something is supposed to happen when the Word is preached.

Louder, the Lord said to me, "PREACH!" I stood there and preached until they said all they could see was a ball of light standing there before them. I preached until they said they couldn't hear my voice. After the microphone was packed away ten thousand people were still hearing my voice. The Glory of God carries your voice. You don't have a voice without having a realm, and a realm isn't void of a voice. God told me to preach and I preached like I'd never preached before. A leg came from nowhere. I'm not talking one or two-inch miracle. I'm talking about two feet of flesh and bone growing out where it had never been.

God said to me, *"In the days ahead you are going to see what people call preaching is not real preaching. There's never a time when you preach that the Heavens don't open. I have to open the Heavens to testify of what I'm saying. I have to confirm it. I don't confirm what I have not said."*

God is not going to confirm your bylaws or your tradition. He's going to confirm what He said. I'm here to tell you that two feet grew out of nowhere. I left the platform, not watching the miracle because I was looking up. My mother in the Lord said to me, "Renny, you know why that happened?" I said, "Well, aside from God showing up, that's about all I know."

She said to me, *"In Africa they have a spirit world. They know good from evil and they know when somebody has it or not. In the West, there is a spirit realm the church does not want to walk in. It's convenient Christianity. We want to modernize it and make it so intellectual that it's nice and good. We sing out of our hymnbook and if something happens, so be it. We've sung our song, read our Scripture, prayed our prayer, had our announcements and our closing prayer, and that was church. Religion is now an item but nothing is happening. Renny do not let anybody fool you with what God just did in your life. I know you've seen miracles, but don't let anyone deceive you concerning your shortcomings."*

Religion never accepts change, because it is against change. This is God? If anybody disturbs the status quo, in your mind, they have upset the boat. God sent them to enlarge your comfort zone.

Can you understand why when Jesus came His choice word was repent? If the minister says the word "repent", the church thinks everybody is in sin. Do you know you don't have to be in sin to repent? The renewal of the mind is affected by repentance. So if you aren't prepared to change, in essence, you are refusing the new thought pattern as it comes to your mind. The word repentance just doesn't mean to change; it means to turn around. How do you turn around from something you've known all your life? You hold on to the old and make that your God.

When God says, *"You know I'm a little more than that. I've got more for you. Let Me invade your space and see another facet of Me."*

God wants to take you higher. What is the point of getting a breakthrough only to go backward?

Chapter Thirteen: Breakthrough

****

"Step out of the boat."

****

Most of you have witnessed miracles, but are you willing to admit that you want to see more manifestations than you are seeing now? If not, you're at that place where you are no longer hungry. Don't be content there. Dig deep and push beyond where you've been. Peter saw signs, wonders and miracles. He saw every miracle you could name, but when he saw Jesus walking on the water, he perceived there was another realm that he hadn't experienced before. Peter stepped out of religion; he stepped out of his boat. It's daunting to step out of the boat if you are the first one stepping out. When the majority sits, criticizes and questions whether or not the move is God, it is difficult. That's why any time God is getting ready to do something new, He uses forerunners of a realm.

Some years ago, when the Holy laughter began, not everyone grasped it. Because it didn't start in their church first, they didn't approve it. We can take months, or years, to step into something God has been doing for quite a while. You can hear it in someone's voice when they are stagnant. No matter how convincing their words, you can tell when they are not growing. Let's focus on growing in the realm of the Spirit and moving on. All Peter wanted to know is this: If it's God, I want it. I'm not saying everyone with you will want the NEW along with you. Just make sure it's God, and when you find out it is God, put your foot out and He'll make the waters solid under your feet. He will use you as an example so those around you will see and know this is a move of God. This move is for anyone daring to step up higher. Say it with me, "I'm going to step up higher." Do you know what happens when you step up higher? Your legs start to dangle. When your legs start to dangle, they are not touching anything familiar. There's a new realm.

Tradition has no problem with history because history is past tense. It is in a box. It is safe. We embrace it, and in turn, doctrines are born. Everyone reverts to tradition, however you must decide if you're going to live by tradition, or faith. If you're going to move in the now—that's faith. If you want to stay in the past—that's tradition. Tradition hasn't grown and it hasn't moved on. God is so much more than what you know. Everything new is measured by something that is lifeless. A new doctrine never brings a move of God. When young people

147

come into the church and you give them doctrine, you run them out of the church. What they want is Jesus in the now. If it isn't in the now, they don't want it. They do not want 1950, 1960, 1970, 1980, or even 1990. They want the now.

The Bible is a complex book to interpret. Some things we just can't interpret. You have to ask the Holy Spirit to reveal it to you. A vocabulary was used then that would not even make sense today. You couldn't even understand some of the things they said then because today, there may not be a word for it in our language. Tradition doesn't understand a word in the now. There are some things you would say that wouldn't cause an offense, but go to another setting, and say that same thing and see the reaction from the people who hear it. They misunderstand your application entirely. You interpret something that Brother so-and-so didn't even say because you are measuring the speaker with your 1950's meaning of the word. It doesn't mean that now because the meaning of a word, and the truth, are two separate things.

Young people will tell you what they feel while they are hurting.

Truth is an absolute. You can't negotiate with it. That's why the Bible speaks about coming to the knowledge of the truth. And, if you stop at 1950-1980, you've stopped coming to the knowledge of the truth. When you stop coming to the knowledge of the truth, you will no longer have the manifestation of the "now faith". That's why Peter spoke about the present-day truth. If I came to minister to you and said what you're used to hearing, it would be an insult. Caleb, my son, is thirteen at this writing, and I'm aware of his intelligence growing. When a child is developing, you change your words to fit his or her level of intelligence. Speak beneath him and the child misunderstands you. Children today say, "Mommy and Daddy don't think I understand." It is because you are speaking beneath their level of intelligence. If someone speaks to you beneath your intellect, you're insulted. What they're actually saying by their actions is that you are not growing. You don't speak to a person who just got saved as you would when they are ten or twenty years in the faith.

It was like that with Paul when he met with the brethren. He said in the book of Hebrews, "When I came here to see you guys, you ought to be at the place where I am teaching, but now you need to be taught again." I have paraphrased this one sentence for you.

"For when for the time ye ought to be teachers, ye have need that one teach you again which be the first principles of the oracles of God; and are become such as have need of milk, and not of strong meat." (Hebrews 5:12)

If I pat you on the head and keep you under my thumb and speak to your one level, you will never grow.

The Bible says, *"My people are destroyed for lack of knowledge."* (Hosea 4:6)

You can't grasp this if you just want to hear a John 3:16 and a John 4. Jesus is coming for a church that is mature—a church that's supposed to be eating meat.

Women know that children are weaned from the breast at different ages. Every child's maturation is different. If we believe Jesus is coming, and we are living in the last days, we should understand that children who are birthed into the church today comprehend more of the Spirit than those who have been sitting in the church for years. Kids are quicker to understand the realm of the Spirit, because they haven't been through religion, and they don't have any garbage to wade through. I've always preferred to start churches with people who have never been saved. They're the easiest ones to disciple. Observe the spiritual bullfrog who knows every church in town. Check him out. He will compare you to the first pastor and the second pastor. If you have discernment, then you should ask him, "What are you doing here?" If it was so good there, why in the world did you leave? Tradition stifles your growth, and as a result, you stop coming to the knowledge of the truth.

For example, I met a friend I hadn't seen in years. He said, "You look so good. You've changed." I said, "That's wonderful, isn't it?" He said, "No." I hadn't seen him since I was twelve. I said, "What do you want me to do—skip, dance, cry or what?" He said, "You've just changed." Do you notice we really don't appreciate it when people change for the better? We can't accept it because they are no longer the same. Tradition has no problem with history because history has already happened. It is not in the now. It's not God that upsets people; they believe in God.

What upsets them is religion. We Pentecostals are no different from the traditionalist because when we cease to grow, we revert to our traditions. Today's youth will not abide what we did in the fifties, because they have the discernment to question it. Where we merely accept it, they inspect it. If they don't think it's creditable they will have nothing to do with it. It's not good enough to say, "That's the way my grandma did it and we don't question it." It worked back then but it's not working now. Is this faith? If the enemy can keep you out of the now, he will. He hates it. Can you imagine when you get unclogged and your faith begins to flow? A double-minded man is either or neither because a double-minded man doesn't really know. But when you start to know, you are considered rebellious.

Jesus was raised in the synagogue. When He was asked to read the Jewish scroll, He read where the last person stopped. Was this coincidence? Jesus had received the Holy Ghost and entered the synagogue, and the attendant said, "Will you please read the Scriptures for us?" There are two seats in the synagogue: one for the rabbi and one for the Messiah. How can it be coincidental that the next Scripture was, "The Spirit of the Lord is upon Me." Jesus was reading from the book of Isaiah and sat down in the Messiah seat. Jesus found Himself in the book. When you know who you are, religion does not intimidate you. The service continued as usual, but the old priesthood didn't embrace this change.

****

"God is going to shift some mantles."

****

When Jesus died, He left another clue. There is a Jewish custom that Jesus followed, and they didn't even know it was Him. In a Jewish household if I eat a meal with you and I like your food, I'll fold the napkin at the end of the meal. That means I am coming back. The Bible says that upon entering the tomb, they found His clothes folded. That's why some believed. They understood the sign. Jesus left every possible clue, but most of them missed God. It is possible, as much as we are enjoying ourselves, to miss the next realm of God. Jerusalem was judged—not because they lacked revelation or prophecy—because they couldn't discern the time. When you discern your hour of visitation, your days in the wilderness are over. When you can discern your visitation, your days of struggling have come to an end. The devil loves it when you ignore this move of God, and you stay in the boat. When the visitation comes, you can really miss what God is doing if you are taking it for granted. When you take it lightly, you'll find that God will take this move to another place. It's a wake-up call for the church. Some of you struggle because you've exhausted the realm of the

Spirit in which you are living. God has something higher but until you shed the old, you cannot receive the new. The miracles we are seeing in the Glory is just the tip of the iceberg, not the fullness.

Expect God to do something totally different. God is going to shift some mantles. Disobedience can cause His hand to switch. I know there's an outburst coming, such as the Toronto movement. It can happen anywhere things shift into place. If we obstruct it, we can miss it. Just allow God to have His way. Can you see how it is possible to stop growing and not know it? You can tell you are not growing when your diet stays the same. We need a change of diet. The French have coffee and bread for breakfast, and they don't accept dietary changes. In the fivefold ministry, the last gift revealed in the Bible was the apostolic. The prophetic was established from the old. The apostolic ministry was given last because it brings order. The church has been mired in a pastoral mantle to the degree that is all it can digest. That's why we are full of teachers in the West. Everybody likes that nice three-point sermon. You have your religion, and you go home to business as usual. We have accepted the evangelist, but we are not accustomed to the full-blown prophet.

Prophecy necessitates a period of time. In the Glory of God there is no time period. Paul even wrote that tongues are going to cease (I Corinthians 13). Prophecy will cease because everything is in the Glory of God where there is no time period. We're nearing the end of time. The period of time for prophecy to be fulfilled is narrowing. What would normally take six months is going to take a month. What would take a month is going to take a week. What would take a week is going to take a day. It's been documented, a scientific fact that the speed of light is slowing down. This is reality.

Faith is dispensational, meaning it is for a revealed period of time. It is the revealed now. Revelation is also dispensational. If faith and revelation are dispensational, do you realize that time can be added through revelation? The revealed truth can cause time to be supplemented. Jesus is coming, and what He does, He will do quickly. The Bible says He will pour His Spirit out on all flesh.

"And it shall come to pass afterward, that I will pour out my spirit upon all flesh; and your sons and your daughters shall prophesy, your old men shall dream dreams, your young men shall see visions: And also upon the

servants and upon the handmaids in those days will I pour out my spirit."
(Joel 2:28-29)

The outpouring is only for a certain period of time. The Feast of Tabernacles is not an outpouring. Joel never named the day. He said it would come to pass. Joel saw the entirety of the beginnings that Peter saw on the day of Pentecost. Peter said, "This is that." It was Joel's prophecy being fulfilled. God declares the end from the beginning and the beginning from the end (Isaiah 46:10). We are almost out of time. We're nearly at the end of the sixth day. "Last days" means two days. The other realm—the Glory realm—will cover the earth. The difference between the previous realm and this realm is revelation. The Bible says the Glory is a realm that is to be revealed (I Peter 5:1). If it's revelation that's being revealed, then through revelation knowledge God can add time to fulfill what He's called you to do. In one week God can allow you to do what would have taken fifty years to accomplish. Now you know why the book of Isaiah says, "What is this that Zion brings forth in the same day?"

> *"Who hath heard such a thing? who hath seen such things? Shall the earth be made to bring forth in one day? or shall a nation be born at once? for as soon as Zion travailed, she brought forth her children."* (Isaiah 66:8)

Many of you have been pregnant with the purposes and callings of God but your time has not yet come. Given that you are part of the end, God will restore the years that the locust ate. Can you imagine all the years when you couldn't walk now being restored? Now you know why Satan hates revelation knowledge. Time is being added, while the devil's time is being shortened. That's why whenever I hear that someone has a revelation of the Glory of God I want to hear it.

In the Feast of Tabernacles there is a day called... "in the hour you think not."

> *"Therefore be ye also ready: for in such an hour as ye think not the Son of man cometh."* (Matthew 24:44)

That's how I can tell Jesus is not coming in this outpouring. Jesus is not coming the way you think. He's coming in the hour you think not. That's not part of Pentecost; it's part of Tabernacles. It means as the world is being filled with the revelation of the Glory of God, Jesus will come. Matthew says that He is going to appear in Glory.

"... They shall see the Son of man coming in the clouds of heaven with power and great glory." (Matthew 24:30)

The Feast of Tabernacles symbolizes the Glory realm of God. What was a fifty-day feast, God turned into 2,000 years. But this last feast it is not going to last 2,000 years.

Do you know what God is going to do in the next year of your life? Everything you lost, everything that was not working for you will be restored. Do you know that in the Glory realm of God you don't age? Can you imagine when your hair starts to grow back, or your teeth start to grow back, like the woman in Pennsylvania? Your biological clock does not affect the Glory of God. The realm comes down and stays. God is going to restore to the church the years it has lost. In the anointing you can burn out. The anointing of God is the outpouring for work. It is power for service. Living in the presence of God is not the display of a gift. In the Glory of God, you rest. Energy is not being used. In the anointing you do the work. In the Glory it is all Him. When we learn to live in the presence of God, our work becomes easy. From the outpouring to the Glory, our youth is renewed. We rest.

"But they that wait upon the LORD shall renew their strength; they shall mount up with wings as eagles; they shall run, and not be weary; and they shall walk, and not faint." (Isaiah 40:31)

Renny McLean

CHAPTER FOURTEEN

Knowledge of The Glory

"Science without religion is lame, religion without science is blind."
-Albert Einstein

There are multiple realms being added to our services and we should be very sensitive to them.

"Let us therefore fear, lest, a promise being left us of entering into his rest, any of you should seem to come short of it. For unto us was the gospel preached, as well as unto them: but the word preached did not profit them, not being mixed with faith in them that heard it. For we which have believed do enter into rest, as he said, As I have sworn in my wrath, if they shall enter into my rest: although the works were finished from the foundation of the world." (Hebrews 4:1-3)

As we lay a foundation to afford you a better working knowledge of the Glory realm, the issue is not the measure of your faith. The issue is who is really speaking? We must discern the difference from confession and declaration. The word, declare means to bring something forward (to announce, predict, proclaim, explain). So, you don't have to wait for December to come. Why? Because when you declare a thing, you are bringing something forward that should occur in its natural time. However, in the realm of the Spirit there is no time. In the realm of the Spirit, we must discern that time is virtually at an end and you don't have to wait until the end to believe God for the fulfillment of great things. My Bible says, "The end from the beginning and the beginning from the end."

"Declaring the end from the beginning, and from ancient times the things that are not yet done, saying, My counsel shall stand, and I will do all my pleasure." (Isaiah 46:10)

When you begin flowing in the Glory of God, your level of faith begins to change. You learn that it is not necessarily the level of faith that brings the miracle when your faith brings you to the realm where things have already happened. It is not your faith that is trying to make something happen because you are in a realm where it already exits. Since we are still programmed to think according to time, we can miss something that truly is for now. I am not talking about a confession or how much faith you have.

In the Garden of Eden Satan didn't say to Eve, "How much faith do you have?" If God said something, your measure of faith doesn't have a bearing. The question is this: Is God bigger than you? He does not need faith to be God. He is God. If God is really speaking, we have to believe that no word that comes from the Throne is "next year".

Look at the way doctors treat you. They put a time limit on your condition— "in the next six months." We are pre-programmed and set to the word of a man. Hence, setting a time gets in the way of a miracle. Faith isn't the issue. The real issue is: "Did God really say it?" If God said it, you can go before God and say, "God, You said this."

The Bible says in Numbers 23:19 (KJV) *"God is not a man, that he should lie; neither the son of man, that he should repent: hath he said, and shall he not do it? or hath he spoken, and shall he not make it good?"*

The Word did not profit them because it was not mixed with faith.

"For unto us was the gospel preached... not being mixed with faith in them that heard it. For we which have believed do enter into rest." (Hebrews 4:2)

There is a difference between hearing and understanding. There is a difference between moving in faith and moving in the Glory of God. When faith is working in you, you know it. It is a gift imparted and when that gift is working you know it. There are times when God is not moving in your life. Faith wasn't an issue. You weren't even looking for it.

Faith's reward is not necessarily a miracle. What is faith's fulfillment? It is entering into the presence of God. When that happens, you are not doing it any more. You are in a world where nothing is being created. Because the Heavens are perfect, there is nothing you lack or need; the earth right now is in a prophetic drama. Heaven is the realm where it has already happened. It is not going to happen. It has already happened. Yet, in the earth it has not happened as yet.

When man was thrown out of the Glory of the Garden, he lost his position in the Glory realm. He fell short of the Glory.

"For all have sinned and come short of the glory of God." (Romans 3:23)

He lost the ability to walk in the manifest presence of God.

It is possible to be in a place where you see great faith, but you don't necessarily feel the Glory. You must discern the difference between the faith realm and the Glory of God. Grace is the glove of faith. Simply put, it is not how much you have or what you can do. Grace is given because it is already done. When you divorce grace from faith, you have a doctrine of works, and that is when you think that it is your gift that brings the miracle. You need to discern the manifestation of the gifts from the Glory of God. According to 1 Corinthians 12, all the gifts have a foundation in faith. You prophesy and move in miracles according to your proportion of faith.

"Having then gifts differing according to the grace that is given to us, whether prophecy, let us prophesy according to the proportion of faith; (Romans 12:6)

In a faith realm, the gifts never come to their maximum because the faith realm is the realm of substance. It is the realm of beginning. In the Glory of God, you see the maximum of the manifestation of the gifts of the Spirit. In the Glory it doesn't take two gifts to bring forth a manifestation. For example, tongues and interpretation are equal to prophesying. You cannot say they are prophecy; they are equal to prophecy. Why are the two listed separately? Speaking in tongues builds your faith to say the prophetic word. You have the word before you speak in tongues. But you speak in tongues to build your faith to interpret the word. When you are in the Glory, it is the very atmosphere of God's presence that carries the utterance inside you. It is not your faith. You just prophesy.

The Bible tells us in Hebrews 4 about entering that place of rest. When you enter the Glory of God, the gifts operate at their maximum, not their minimum.

It is for this reason I was criticized profusely. In our meetings, people would start getting healed. Sometimes you would miss the mass miracle because you concentrated on the one that is being healed. That person made a demand on your gift, and you stopped to minister to that one. Unless you go further, the others fail to receive because you are involved with only one.

The woman with the issue of blood made a demand of the anointing on Jesus. In many local churches this is where the pastor has problems. When an apostolic, and/or prophetic gift, or evangelist comes to the church, the people put a demand on the speaker's gifts. The expectancy of the people is higher.

If the pastor is not growing in the revelation of God, it is because the people do not put the same demand on her or him. Believers, at times, can assume the pastor just doesn't have it. In reality, it is because you do not put the same demand on them that you do on the guest speaker. The believer has become event orientated regarding the supernatural, rather than it being the life of Christ manifested in the Church. When you put a demand on the pastor, they will grow overnight, because your faith is pulling the manifestation resident in their spirit. This is why the church can come to a place where the pastor feels like he or she is burning out. Why? People are no longer pulling from their pastor, and when the people are no longer pulling, the service can become a drag. The fivefold must be called upon for their gifts to be of benefit to the church. If the body does not call upon these offices and giftings, then they will be the ones to lose out on all of the benefits in them.

That is why, at times, when you go where there is no knowledge of your ministry, nothing happens. In Matthew's account of the gospel, Jesus went to his own city where He was well known. He healed only a few sick.

"And he could there do no mighty work, save that he laid his hands upon a few sick folk, and healed them." (Mark 6:5)

But when they had knowledge of Him, they brought the sick and the possessed and all were healed. These are the basics of the faith of God and the anointing of the Holy Spirit.

But we must not overlook the fact that the media now gives us an edge that the early church did not possess. The tools we have to spread the Word of God are so much greater than we could even imagine. The real key to the success of using these tools is what we do with them. What is our motivation for using them? Accountability is something we must all take into consideration in using the media to advertise our meetings. When we do not have the finances to let the entire community know about a meeting, we must trust that God is indeed the One who knows all about the situation. I have adopted a phrase over the years which helps me keep the success of any meeting in check. It goes like this; "We are not in the Book of Numbers, we are in the Book of Acts."

All too often we come to church, and it seems as if the service never fully enters into the manifested presence of God. We often accept an atmosphere of worship as the fullness of God after something has happened. It might be a message in tongues, a word of wisdom, or a miracle. After a while, no matter how good it is, the service becomes monotonous. There is no revelation of Christ in the midst in order to perpetuate the manifestation of His presence. Without that revelation, there is no manifestation. When you pitch a tent and set up camp where you are, God moves on, leaving you worshiping the residue of His last visitation. What we lose sight of is that His cloud of Glory has moved on, and we are missing out on what the new thing He is doing.

The Bible tells us that Jacob went to bed one night and dreamed. He woke up and the manifestation of the presence of God had left him. He said, "God was in this place, and I didn't know it."

"And Jacob awaked out of his sleep, and he said, Surely the LORD is in this place; and I knew it not." (Genesis 28:16)

God had moved on. When Jacob awoke, all he had was the residue of the visitation. Without the revelation there is no acceleration of the manifestation. There is a principle of creativity in every revelation of God.

You must understand there is a difference between a follower of the ark and a carrier of the ark. God is raising people up to carry the ark. You must learn how to carry the ark for yourself. It is not about carrying another person's ark. You will be blessed, and you will receive from others, but if you don't have the ark yourself you can't carry it. When you go into a place to minister, your spirit acts out of the atmosphere which is in that place. Because your spirit never forgets an atmosphere, your spirit also knows how to recreate one. That can be good or bad. If you settle for an atmosphere where the realm of the worship is not revealing the manifestation of the Glory, and if you decide that atmosphere is the one you want to minister in, from that day on you have just set the limit on yourself and your ministry. If you listen when someone is speaking, you can actually see, with your eyes of faith, into the realm from where the words are coming. It is then you know if the word being spoken is full of life or death. What that person is saying is actually coming from a vessel with knowledge. It is not about confession just to make it look good. It is about what God is really saying. If God said it, it will come to pass.

"For unto us was the gospel preached, as well as unto them: but the word preached did not profit them, not being mixed with faith in them that heard it." (Hebrews 4:2)

Because the Word was not mixed with faith, it did not profit them. There are some things you can impart through the laying on of hands but there are some things you cannot impart. Many need to discern when Heaven is open over them. While some people are receiving, because they have learned how to receive, each one of us needs to learn how to receive from the realm of Glory. Until you learn how to open Heaven for yourself, you cannot carry the ark. There is a level of revelation, understanding and reverence necessary for one to carry the ark of His presence.

Let me give you a better idea as to how we fail to gain access into that level of relationship where we are trusted with the deeper things of God. I want to address those in ministry here, if you will allow me to do so. When you exit a meeting where you have received an impartation and you start ministering, you won't know how to bring that manifestation. In order to bring this Word throughout the world, you must have the revelation of how to administrate it. Again, there are those who follow and there are those who carry. Many are called, but few are chosen. The accountability factor is always at the cutting edge of anyone's walk with God.

****

"A dispensation is a revealed period of time."

****

Allow me to share a truth with you. The average believer has difficulty remaining in the manifested presence of God. Many do not even know how to get there. When the average believer comes into a meeting where there is an open Heaven and somebody disturbs them, they lapse into the flesh by reacting to the situation and not the atmosphere. Do not be confused by the differences I am referring to here. I am not talking about simply getting the blessings, but about remaining in that realm from whence the blessings came from. When you are here on earth, you live by faith. But, when you are there, in the Glory realm, nothing should disturb you. You are in this world but not of it. Your body is here but the real you is not here.

The renewal of your mind is dispensational. A dispensation is a revealed period of time. The dispensation of time is the now of God. That is the prophetic faith. In other words, when you look at the phrase "it was", it actually means now. What the Spirit is saying is revealed for now. When someone speaks after-the-fact concerning events, they are speaking historically, not prophetically.

In Romans 12:2, the message is "Do not be conformed to this age." There is another time zone that bypasses the one where you live. You are really from the eternal, and because you are from there, you have an eternal conscientiousness. Once you are there, you can't get caught up in what is happening here.

It is more real to you up there than here; and here doesn't mean too much because you are really up there. You realize that the devil is trying to reduce you to accepting a lower position here in order to keep you here.

Ponder this for a moment. Are you a human being having a supernatural experience? Or are you a Spirit being having a human experience? This helps you to view the perspective in a more proper manner. The supernatural is another realm altogether.

We must come to maturity in the Spirit where we stop limiting God. When we really see God, not through the eyes of tradition or our culture, we will give Him His rightful place. Long ago when the church had meetings where nothing happened, folks would say, "Wasn't that good?" And you would say, "Who was healed?" Nobody! "Who was delivered?" Nobody! "Who was set free?" Someone would give you a nice emotional word, but nothing really happened. But we knew something took place. It was just that we were unable to articulate what it was that happened.

If we really believe that Jesus is coming, we must understand the supernatural realm. We will be caught up in what is happening here. I don't even care about what is coming. My Bible says, "When you see these things, look up!" You are not to look at the things on the earth. When you keep looking at the things here you conform to what you are looking at here.

When you conform you will adopt their school of thought. Why? How can you be in the presence of God, who is all-powerful, and be fearful? If we give God His place and let Him be God, our lives will never be the same.

"For unto us was the gospel preached, as well as unto them: but the word preached did not profit them, not being mixed with faith in them that heard it." (Hebrews 4:2)

The Scripture said it did not profit them because it was not mixed with faith. Moses knew God's ways but his people only knew God's works. When God does something, you rejoice. When He doesn't, you are back to here (the earth realm).

"For we which have believed do enter into rest, as he said, As I have sworn in my wrath, if they shall enter into my rest: although the works were finished from the foundation of the world." (Hebrews 4:3)

The works were finished from the foundation of the world. "It is finished," were Jesus' words from the cross. For forty years the children of Israel were in the wilderness walking around seeing the supernatural acts of God. Prior to their wilderness, He gave them a sneak preview. He sent plagues to the Egyptians, yet the Israelites were covered and protected from every plague.

When it was their time to be free to walk into the wilderness, you would think that a miracle wouldn't be a problem. But it was, because they didn't learn how to live supernaturally. We are at a time in history where we are being pushed into the arena of miracles, whether you know how to flow in it or not.

God has created circumstances that are coming to the earth, and the supernatural move of God will be the only thing that sustains us. It is not about getting someone else's experience. The more you clone the less quality there is. We're all unique. We have to know God for ourselves. Nothing can shake you or move you if you know Him for yourself.

You would have thought that the mindset of the Israelites would have been, "If He did it before He will do it again. When we get to this place in our life, we shouldn't question God. He has delivered us and set us free." You have proved it time and time again. Why should the things that are designed to move the world move you?

Paul said in Acts 20:24 (KJV) *"But none of these things move me, neither count I my life dear unto myself, so that I might finish my course with joy, and the ministry, which I have received of the Lord Jesus, to testify the gospel of the grace of God."*

The church was born in adverse circumstances. If God looked after the church, then, He will do it now. Just be sure there is some blood on your doorpost. This is the Word of God. Jesus is coming and we must learn how to walk in the supernatural as a lifestyle. You don't have to struggle to believe. This one thing I know is that He is able!

Renny McLean

CHAPTER FIFTEEN

Knowing the Realm

"The men of experiment are like the ant,
they only collect and use;
the reasoners resemble spiders,
who make cobwebs out of their own substance.
But the bee takes the middle course.
It gathers its material from the flowers of the garden
and field, but transforms
and digests it by a power of its own.
Not unlike science, this is the true business of
philosophy for it neither relies solely or
chiefly on the powers of the mind,
nor does it take the matter which it
gathers from natural history and
mechanical experiments and lay up in the
memory whole, as it finds it, but lays it up
in the understanding altered and digested.
Therefore, from a closer and purer league
between these two faculties,
the experimental and the rational
(such as has never been made),
much may be hoped"
-Francis Bacon

I had the feeling that there was a miracle for which God had not yet given me the word of knowledge on. In another meeting, the Lord said, "Declare the creative miracle." Everyone experienced the manifested presence of God on their bodies. One lady said to me, "Renny, you must understand that in the Glory of God there is no time period for growth. That's why when you get into the Glory, miracles are instantaneous. In a faith realm it can take some time. Nothing's wrong with faith, you understand, just make sure you get your miracle either way."

We closed that service at twelve o'clock midnight and I had been on the platform since seven. God is moving. Thank God for His presence, but there is something else we have to perceive. I wonder how many miracles really happened in Jesus' ministry. There are only twenty-six miracles recorded in Jesus' ministry.

Do you realize that the average minister that moves in miracles sees more than an average of twenty-six miracles in a night? Not every miracle that Jesus ever performed was recorded. The Bible says that if everything Jesus did was recorded, all the books in the world could not contain it.

Prior to the initial appearance of the gold dust, we had witnessed the supernatural oil manifesting in our meetings. That was not new to us. I said, "Lord, tell me something about unusual signs."

He said, *"It is nothing more than a sign and a wonder, Renny. With this manifestation there are some things you don't explain. It is a sign and wonder."*

You can't explain it to the carnal man but the spiritual man knows it is God. To people who don't really discern what the Spirit wants to do right now, it's an enigma.

He said, *"Renny, the time has come in the realm of the Spirit where the unseen will no longer remain unseen."*

We have spoken about the riches in Glory but the time has come when you are literally going to see the riches in Glory. Yes, we are going to see it. If it's there, we are going to see it.

The most common questions in 1999 were concerning the Y2k bug. When asked about it, God reenacted a vision He gave me in 1989. I saw the earth spinning. To the right of the earth I saw the scales of God. I saw them every time God spoke about a change about to take place. He said, "Don't take your eyes off of it. Just look." When one part of the scale went down, there were people on top of the scale as it tipped downward. But when the opposite side of the scales arose, there were people experiencing an incredible transference of wealth.

I believe we are in the hour when the wealth transference is going to occur. Why? We have been in the 'last days" for 2,000 years. But prophetically speaking, we have only been in the "end times" since 1948. From 1948 to 1998 is fifty years. What is happening now, in 2004? Joel's prophecy is being fulfilled. Do you know that the Glory of God is dispensational (for a revealed period of time)? It is. If the end time started at 1948, where does that position us now? This is a realm that is being revealed.

We're familiar with the anointing. We know about the faith realm. Faith is written. Look in the Bible. It actually tells you about a "realm being revealed." The Bible says that it will come to pass that the earth will be filled with the knowledge of the Glory of the Lord as the waters cover the sea.

*"For the earth shall be filled with the knowledge of the glory of the LORD, as the waters cover the sea." (*Habakkuk 2:14)

We are chasing the Glory but the Bible says there is knowledge of the Glory, and right now, this knowledge is being revealed. When you begin a service, it is difficult to know what you are going to preach, unless you speak what you have always spoken.

When the Glory is present, it removes the stress from preaching. It is another world. Your missing body part is in that realm. At times you have entered the Glory of God but you left without the body part you needed. Man was not created in the faith realm. Man was made in the Glory of God. That is why everything you need, everything you are, is in the Glory of God. When you are in the Glory, there is no time.

Scientists made a discovery that should make us think. They discovered that the speed of light is slowing down. We are coming out of a time zone and we are entering into the eternal realm. In the eternal realm your body clock is different. There are times when you are sick and surgeons will remove one part of your body and replace it. You have heard of liver or kidney transplants. Sometimes people die when they have had a transplant. Maybe it was not your body that rejected it. Maybe your spirit rejected it because your spirit knows that God can recreate it.

We must understand that this creative realm is valid. It is not a faith realm where we have to stir it up to get it. If you get in the presence of God, your eardrums are there. Your new eyes are there. Your bones are there. If you really get in the Glory of God and stay there, your missing body part will form of its own accord.

I have been in places where people in a faith realm receive more miracles than those who walk in a Glory realm. Because they have knowledge of the faith realm, they know how to maximize it. If you do not have that same level of knowledge, there are manifestations you can miss.

****

"Faith is the foundation for the access into the Glory of God."

****

Can you imagine having the same revelation of the Glory that you do of faith? Some people have knowledge of the Glory but none of the faith realm. They can live in the Glory but when trouble comes, you can't stay there if you have no foundation. Faith is the foundation for the access into the Glory of God.

At one revival meeting in the Midwest, I was praying for the pastor to carry the revival after I left. As I touched him, I saw Jacob's ladder. I saw the pastor going up the ladder. Each time he ascended, God removed the rungs of the ladder. I said to him, "The Lord wants you to know that where you are going there are no steps for you to come back down." It is time that we quit having the up-and-down experience, the in-and-out experience.

If we are in the Glory realm, we had better stay there. If we stay in the Glory the enemy's not a problem because he's not there. Some of you are staying in the realm where he is. These people are huffing and puffing, fighting the fight of faith. They haven't learned to enter God's rest. When you enter the rest of God, you know the victory is yours, but the battle is the Lord's. He wants you to stay before His face and praise Him. As you praise Him, you're unaware of what is going on around you because the atmosphere changes when you praise.

Recently, when I was stuck at the airport, I felt the anointing of a Pentecostal temper for the first time in years. I felt led to lay hands on somebody.

Sometime later, while (finally) in flight, God spoke to me. "Renny, do you notice that when you are in the air you are not conscious of the plane's speed when it is in its height. You are only conscious of speed the more you descend."

In that same way, you are only conscious of your disease, sickness, or debt because of where you live. You don't want to go higher. When you go higher you learn that your circumstance can't come where you are going. If God can get you in the Glory realm, Satan can't come there with you. He can stay right where he is because earth is his territory. But the Glory realm is not his territory. The higher we ascend, the less we are aware of ourselves. All of you were healed long before it manifested in time.

Renny McLean

CHAPTER SIXTEEN

The Supernatural Realm of the Spirit

"Science has yet to explain the most remarkable creation in the world - the human brain"
-Loren C. Eiseley
Professor of Anthropology, University of Pennsylvania

There are three realms of the supernatural: the faith realm, the realm of the anointing, and the realm of Glory of God. There are times we say this is the anointing when it is actually the Glory. Consider the Jewish feasts: Passover represents faith. Pentecost represents the anointing and Tabernacles represents the Glory of God. God made man to live in the Glory of God.

When man sinned (and all have sinned and come short of the Glory of God), man fell short of the Glory. God gave man the next best thing. God had to anoint man down through the ages. In the beginning, man lived in the Glory of God. The anointing accomplishes several things. It convicts us of sin and unrighteousness; it makes you alive in His presence and empowers you to stand.

God anointed prophets, priests and kings. Without the anointing the priest could not stand in the Holy Place. We are familiar with the expressions of faith and of the anointing. The highest realm of God is His Glory. God is calling the church to walk in His Glory. Thank God for the faith realm, but faith is the substance.

God is calling us to walk in His fullness. There are some things that are going to radically change in the life of the church. The current is changing. In the realm of the Spirit, there's a difference between seeing and perceiving. Anyone can look but not everyone can perceive. When you are in the realm of the

Heavens you perceive, and you know. Have you ever known something in the natural, but you didn't know how you knew? You didn't need anyone to explain it or give you a doctrine for it. It's that way in the realm of the Spirit.

Often our stinking thinking gets in the way of the Spirit. If we can't reason it, we say it's not God. This mentality impedes perceiving God. In reading the Major Prophets, you often hear this word: "The word of the Lord came unto me saying and I saw. . ." In the realm of the Spirit, we can describe what we are seeing. However, there are no words for some things in the Spirit. Paul saw some things he couldn't speak about. There are some things in God's Glory that we cannot describe.

For instance, there is no word to fully explain agape love. A word is nothing more than an idea that we all agree upon. It is the same way in the Spirit. For example, Joshua said to the sun, "Stand still."

By faith, the world was framed by the word.

"Through faith we understand that the worlds were framed by the word of God, so that things which are seen were not made of things which do appear." (Hebrews 11:3)

The faith realm is the spiritual structure of the invisible world. When you perceive something, it becomes set in the realm of time, and then recorded into history. Vision and hearing are the same in the realm of the Spirit. There are manifestations that leave the throne of God constantly, and we miss them.

We must be aware of them to keep them on the earth. The speed of light is quicker than the speed of sound. Are you aware that what we hear has already happened? What we are seeing is what is happening. Manifestations leave the Heavens constantly and they remain here only if we pick them up and declare them. God is looking for the people who will catch the things that He is sending and keep them on the earth. This was spoken to the earth 3,000 years ago. I'm not talking about confession. I'm talking about declaring it. There is a difference between declaring it and confessing it.

In the Word of God, you declare what is revealed. When you name that thing, it is framed. When manifestations come to the earth, you declare it when you see it. This 21st Century church is looking for so much confirmation that by the time you get your confirmation, the manifestation has already left. It does not stay on the earth unless you declare it. The Lord is bringing the church into declaring what we see and keeping it on the earth.

In Revelation 4:1 (KJV) John said, *"After this I looked, and, behold, a door was opened in heaven: and the first voice which I heard was as it were of a trumpet talking with me; which said, Come up hither, and I will shew thee things which must be hereafter. And immediately I was in the spirit."*

John was in the Spirit immediately. How long does it take for you to get there? Sometimes it takes an hour of strong praise to get free and pass over. This is where the church is today. God wants us to come to the place where we no longer need to be stirred up—where we're instantly in the Spirit. If we are there, then our language must change. We cannot speak from Earth's perspective, but with the perspective of the Heavens. Heaven's perspective doesn't speak of getting something to happen. You speak of the thing as it actually is happening. Genesis 1 says the Spirit moved when God spoke (Genesis.1: 2-3).

Speech was originally designed for a response. You speak in response to something that has happened. So, when God said, "Let there be light." The Spirit of the Lord moved. In the mind of God, it was already light. God created the sun and stars on the fourth day. The world knows time because of the sun and the four seasons of the earth.

The speed of light slowed down by the fourth day. Science will verify that the speed of light is slowing down now. They say the speed of light is coming to the time where time will be no more. Creative miracles will become the norm because you are no longer going to look to a time for a limb to grow back. You will realize that when you speak, it will happen at the very moment.

The Spirit realm is easy. Even psychics tap into this realm faster than the church does. They believe in the realm of the Spirit more easily than the church, because in the Body of Christ, we are educated apart from the realm of the Spirit. We are so full of logic that we can't perceive the realm of the Spirit. The realm of the Spirit is neither here nor there. Subconsciously we are taught to live in the realm of the soul. Therefore, we cannot perceive the realm of the Spirit.

The spirit realm is always there. There are things of the Heavens that are constantly being dispersed on the earth, but we are not touching them quickly enough for them to stay here. The manifestations do come but they don't stay on the earth.

When the manifestations came, they were leaving the earth. That is why people only get halfway healed. In a service where the manifestations are moving, it takes God to bring back that moment through praise and worship. The moment was present for someone to be healed or set free. When that moment comes again, you must speak a word in that moment and season. This is the season and time for your miracle. Subconsciously we are trained for the anointed man of God to lay hands on us. The service goes through multiple times and seasons. Our faith is still affixed to the hand of the man. Subconsciously we are trained to put space between ourselves and God. We're trained to believe that it is necessary to have someone lay hands on us. Even though God is in the Heavens, He is next to you. So, if He is right next to you, why wait? He can lay hands on you. You wait because you are programmed to wait. You are preconditioned to wait on things the Bible says are now.

In Ashland, Virginia, the Glory of the Lord came, and I saw people begin to lose weight. I saw that moment in the Spirit. It was as if a balloon was blowing up and God was waiting for me to declare a word. The praise was so strong. I just said, "There are weight losses taking place." At that moment, one woman wrapped her dress around her three times. It was as though God suddenly stuck a pin in the woman and she lost weight. The realm of Glory came; however, I had to declare it.

We are taught that the time to give our offering is when the ushers stand before you. Can we break the time limits we have on ourselves? We are trained to wait and delay things that are now. In the realm of the Spirit, your time to move may not be the same as the person next to you.

There are times in services where all your needs can be met. But we are programmed to respond together. There are times God is meeting your need before the needs of the person next to you. You've got to discern the difference between a personal cloud and a corporate cloud. We must learn how to discern our clouds. There are multiple clouds in the realm of the Spirit. I believe there is a healing cloud, a cloud of prosperity. We need to learn how to create a cloud. Without a cloud there is no rain.

When the Glory was moving the people ran down the aisles to give and they gave their last cent to God. By the time they got back to their seats, the exact amount they gave was back in their pockets! One lady ran down, slapped her money down, and on the way back, the Lord told her to read Psalms 100. She opened her Bible to Psalms 100 and right there was a crisp $100 dollar bill. Her husband verified that she didn't have any money, so it wasn't any money she had forgotten in her Bible. As matter of fact, he said that she'd dropped her Bible several times that evening and nothing fell out. God can grow your money. He can grow your eyeballs, eardrums, skin, and tooth fillings. Believe me, it is real!

****

"The Glory of God is no respecter of disease."

****

Whenever people lose track of time and step into the eternal, the eternal becomes real. God is trying to bridge you from time into the eternal. You will realize the eternal is more real than time. You will find out time is the servant of eternity. Time does exactly what eternity declares it to do. If God has to stop the clock for you to recover your health, He will do it. He can stop the clock for you to restore your limb. The day is coming when we'll have nothing but worship services because all of our needs are met. It's already done!

Praise is an affirmation of God's works, and worship is the affirmation of God's presence. When we come to the knowledge that God is present and moving among us—and time no longer dictates the service—in one moment every sickness can leave an auditorium. The Glory of God is no respecter of disease. The anointing of God is no respecter of diseases.

Let's take our foot off the brakes and understand that the realm of the Spirit is genuine. God is waiting for us to declare what we see. Seeing is not good enough. Declaring it and framing it causes it to stay framed. This is the power of God on the earth. He wants us to declare in the realm of the Spirit what we see in the Heavens. He wants us to keep it here on the earth. God is calling His people to walk in His manifest presence where all our needs are met.

Every camp has its different views. I know when I make this statement it might trouble some folks; nonetheless, it's my humble opinion. If I were ministering to some groups and in one service blind eyes opened, some would say this ministry has an anointing for eyes. If ears were opened, it would be an anointing for the deaf. What if you are in a meeting where everything is healed? I chose to believe it was the Glory of God. I'm not talking of being divinely enabled. I'm talking about when the Glory of God comes in a place and sickness and disease disappear.

The realm of the Spirit, sickness and disease are classified as matter. Sin is classified as matter. The Scriptures are filled with it. It says laying aside every heavy weight that easily besets you.

> *"Therefore, since we are surrounded by such a great cloud of witnesses, let us throw off everything that hinders and the sin that so easily entangles, and let us run with perseverance the race marked out for us."* (Hebrews 12:1) (NIV)

Over the years, I have preached many times on the subject of throwing off those things which hinder us and that so easily entangle us. I want to clarify this Scripture for you in order for you to see what the Spirit is saying about these concepts. First, there is the setting of where this activity takes place. It states that there is a cloud of witnesses surrounding us. Even though these witnesses are watching, they are not like the mythological gods such as Zeus, who could intervene on the behalf of his lesser mortals. These witnesses are there to observe only. Could it be that when the Scripture speaks of us being known as we are known, this observation position has something to do with that process? Will those witnesses be able to speak to us about the races we won or lost? No matter who or what they are, the fact remains that a great many are watching our progress.

Sin is classified as spiritual gravity. Until you get to the root cause of anything there is no change. Until you get to the root cause of what is making you sick, you will remain sick. Until you get to the root cause, the spiritual will support that circumstance and consider it matter you want, instead of matter you don't want. The choice is yours. As Jesus told the woman, "As your faith is, so be it unto you." God is going to get to the root cause of your sickness, disease and infirmity, and the root cause of your debt. He will get to the root cause of drug abuse, not the symptoms, but the cause—the cause of why you get a breakthrough only to go back to where you started.

> *"God, get to the cause! Matter is going to lose its hold if I let God get to the root. There are breakthroughs taking place in my Spirit. I am going to know the root cause and it is being dealt with. I will rest assured, God is getting to the root and I am delivered right now.."*

CHAPTER SEVENTEEN

The Universe of Our Faith

Say these words out loud with me, "Over and Beyond, Beyond and Above" You are about to enter into a new realm of faith. Revelation is going to come to you as never before, concerning the supernatural. The world beyond has gone on, the natural is nothing more than the supernatural slowed down, and the supernatural is nothing more than the natural speeded up, in its original time. We must understand that things are not as they appear. You will need revelation to continue to make withdrawals from the world beyond, because not everything beyond is here now. What is here now, is here by means of a spoken word. That world beyond is so vast it is beyond what we can naturally comprehend. That is why reason cannot comprehend the world beyond.

*"Through faith we understand that the worlds came into being, and still exist, at the command of God, so that what is seen does not owe its existence to that which is visible." (*Hebrews 11:3) (Weymouth Trans.)

'By faith we understand,' meaning perceptive understanding. You have to be able to perceive beyond the natural. Because reason and logic is natural, it does not connect you to the realm of the spirit. It connects you to the natural world. In other words, faith is the ability to believe beyond reason. 'When reason is absent, faith is present.' In other words, reason does not have the ability to comprehend creativity, in its original form. Reason is the determining factor of your unbelief. But faith is over and above reason as we know it.

The unseen universe rules the time universe. Time was created out of eternity and faith speaks from an eternal point of view. So what we see does not determine what a thing is going to be. We call things that are not as though they are. Time does not determine your faith. Faith supersedes the law of time. God can do in one second what would take you a year to do.

The problem is when we speak we speak with a time consciousness. We are the ones who say in six months things are going to happen. We are the ones who are saying the time frame on it. You are speaking from eternity. I want to emphasize to you that there is no time frame in the eternal things of God. Because faith is Now! Now! Now!

****

"Revelation to your spirit man is what common sense is to the natural man."

****

God can heal you now! Yes, your liver can grow back; your bones can grow back, right now! Yes you can turn your faith loose now! See the answer; see the manifestation forming before your spirit man. Believe that. Take your eyes off what the devil has you focused on. Right now! The devil wants you to always see the problem or the situation, but right now you are stepping out of time. All your circumstances are time related. But faith breaks the law of time. Speak the conclusion of the whole matter. I don't need to feel it to know that things are changing right now! Faith believes it and speaks it ahead of time. Time is not the determining factor anymore. But faith is! It is finished, it is done. Live out what you have just said, don't visit the situation in your mind. Renew your mind, the past is gone, it is a new day in your life spiritually, physically, and financially.

There is a physical reality with speaking; until we speak nothing is manufactured from the world beyond. One of the laws of mass that we were taught in science was, not all mass is visible. Faith is the invisible mass from which God creates the seen dimension. That is why it is the substance of things hoped for. Therefore, until we speak nothing is allowed to come from the world beyond without a revealed spoken word.

> *"By faith we understand the ages to have been prepared by a saying of God, in regard to the things seen not having come out of things appearing;"* (Hebrews 11:3) (Youngs Translation)

Revelation to your spirit man is what common sense is to the natural man. Revelation brings elevation, revelation stirs spiritual activity. But, until you speak by faith, miracles don't happen. Because, revelation is the prerequisite to faith, it increases your sphere of influence in the realm of the spirit. A man cannot operate beyond his level of revelation. That is why it is imperative that we come out of our religious boxes and not be controlled anymore by our denominations. We must be willing to associate with others. No camp has all the truths. In fact, most camps have parked in their past truths and have not gone on to current revelation. What has happened spiritual activity begins to wane because, your not moving in a now faith, that has come out of the revealed word.

When faith comes you are not thinking the possibilities in the constraints of time and reason. Reason cannot comprehend revelation, because revelation is from the mind of Christ. Reason is the natural mind, which the Bible says is enmity against God.

"Because the mind of the flesh [is] enmity to God, for to the law of God it doth not subject itself, for neither is it able; and those who are in the flesh are not able to please God." (Romans 8:7-8) (Youngs Translation)

Your natural mind is not able to think on the same level like God. It cannot compute what is beyond it. When faith comes you are not thinking in the constraints of time and reason. Since our reasoning is conformed to the natural, it now becomes the determining factor of our possibilities to the natural man. In other words, it is not based on if a thing is logical. Sometimes people will say that you are crazy if you operate beyond the norm. But, that is what faith is! All things are possible when you believe. Logic keeps you in agreement with the natural world. Revelation is nothing more than the logics of God revealed to man for man to be able to think and to operate out of eternity. The world we speak from is bigger than time itself. Faith is the dominion of the believer over the zone of time.

One of the principles of the spirit realm is that we must understand that the believer is God's agent on the earth, who is authorized by God to declare the things of heaven to the earth. But, as God's agent on the earth we must be in agreement with the Kingdom and Government of God. Heaven stands behind our word and agrees with it coming to pass.

"And I will give to thee the keys of the reign of the heavens, and whatever thou mayest bind upon the earth shall be having been bound in the heavens,

and whatever thou mayest loose upon the earth shall be having been loosed in the heavens.'" (Matthew 16:19) (Youngs Translation)

I am reminded of a lady in Depoe Bay, Oregon who came to our meeting years ago, Margaret was her name. We had been in a series of meetings where all we were speaking on was worship. How in worship we step from time to eternity and the miracles that are in His presence are made available to us. In most cases we don't expect the miracles as we worship. That is why we don't claim them. Your worship will bring you into the glory of God. Like thousands of others, we have seen over the years those who got healed as they worship. Their cancers disappeared; their eyes were healed; their bones were healed; their ears opened; wheelchairs emptied because as we worship, we built the supernatural mass. The miracles are within the mass of His presence, which is known as the glory. We speak into that mass and then the mass takes on the word we speak. The miracles happen. In churches today we are speaking the Word without the mass of God's glory because we don't take time to worship. There is not enough mass in the service to manifest miracles. If you are a preacher, that is the key right there for your ministry. Sister Margaret worshipped, and I remember saying to her, "Rise up and walk." She was in a wheelchair, I did not know that she had plastic hips, and through an unsuccessful operation was unable to walk. The presence of God came in the room, and she stood up by faith. You must respond to the presence of God by faith. Stop questioning or looking around, and focus on Jesus Christ, then the miracles happen. She worshipped, as she stood up she kept worshipping, and she started to walk. Praise God for that miracle, but we only saw the first part of the miracle. When she was taken to hospital and they checked her out, there was no plastic in her hips it had become bone. What a creative miracle! God can create whatever is missing in you. Believe! Right now! And receive!

There are times when we speak the Word we have to keep speaking it because there was not sufficient mass on your word when you spoke it for it to manifest. That is why the Word says we must keep confessing it, and it will come to pass.

CHAPTER EIGHTEEN

Ridding Religious Doctrines

I will never forget what happened to me once when I traveled to a certain country where they knew me, my background, even my eating habits. You cannot guess what meat they cooked. If there was ever a day I had to draw on the fruit of the Spirit I drew deeply that day. If you don't eat, you offend them. If you turn them off, how are they going to sit down and listen to you? You know what I did? I went on my face before God. I said, "If I have to eat pork to win these people then I will do it." Traveling will change you. The problem is we have sat so long behind four walls that we still have religion. The fact that we can't speak to young people in their vernacular shows there is something wrong.

I'm frequently on the road and I really miss seeing my youngest daughter grow. Zoë, age six, is a character unto herself. I told her I would write to her post office box while I was out of town. One day she went to school and tells her teacher about the signs and wonders and Daddy's hands. Zoë said, "Signs and wonders." Her teacher inquired, "Signs and wonders, what signs and wonders?" Zoë told her about the miracles she had seen in Daddy's meetings. Can you imagine if I tried to make Zoë conform? If I were politically correct in raising her, she would never reach her generation. You will never reach your generation if you cannot communicate with them. I don't know some of the lingo this generation speaks. I've tried to listen a few times and I still don't know it. I said, "God, have I been out of touch that long?"

He said, *"No, you've been among My people too long. You need to go out there and hear what they are saying."*

You know what offends the young people? When you are not real with them. If Jesus went into a pub your doctrine would alienate Him. When people come to the church door, they're looking for reality. When you see young people hooked on drugs there is a lack of reality—they're escaping reality. They know reality is out there, but they don't know quite what it is. We are supposed to be what it is. I'm not talking "thou", "thee". They don't know that language. The world doesn't know that language. Ever notice when your doctor speaks to you, half the things he says go way over your head? He'll use those lofty medical terms and then tell you it really means this or that. Why didn't he say that to begin with, instead of giving you a crash course in anatomy?

CHAPTER NINETEEN

What Matters Is the Heart

This is the most exciting time of your life!
You are on the verge of greatness, of glory, of renewed vigor and strength.
You may say the night is upon you, but the day is breaking!

In matters of the heart, there is a troublesome path to understand whether what we sense is reality or the results of a strong toxic lie in which the heart has been taken over by the matter at hand. All through this book we have attempted to drive your attention to the heart of the matter, that being this one, single and powerful truth, "The Spiritual realm holds all matter together." This entire planet, and everything on it and in it, is held in place by the power of His spoken Word. John stunned the early church with a powerful revelation when he spoke in the first chapter of his writing. He declared:

"In the beginning was the Word, and the Word was with God, and the Word was God. The same was in the beginning with God. All things were made by him; and without him was not any thing made that was made. In him was life; and the life was the light of men. And the light shineth in darkness; and the darkness comprehended it not." (John 1:1-5)

You cannot separate God from His Word. The two are one in the same. The Logos and the Rhema are one in Him. The passage of the text which speaks about things being made by Him, and nothing made without Him makes it crystal clear that He was the one doing the creating. He was the one designing. He was the one who spoke into being everything. And everything that He had made responded to His voice print. Before He declared that matter would be, there was no matter. After He made matter, He had the power over His creation to make it do whatever He wanted it to do. Matter was not given the power to choose what it did. It did not have a random access to will. It existed. It waited until it was told what to do by its Creator. Much like a sculptor who walks up to a slab of marble and strikes the very first blow in the process to turn the block of stone into a statue, the marble is just there, waiting for the commanding blow to declare to it what it will become.

It could not get any better, even if it had been given the option, because a perfect Creator had created a perfected thing. Imagine this. No space, then there was space. What was before space? Him! Imagine no constellations, galaxies or black holes. What was before them? Him! Absolutely nothing was made without Him making it. But our fallen intellect rebels against these truths because we cannot imagine something coming out of nothing. Yet when man has an idea, where does it come from? Where did the invention of things by man come from? Out of nothing. They were creative thoughts. Yet out of those ideas came the things we use every day. If man, who has a fallen intellect, which is imperfect, can create things which require the use of the matter He created, then why can we not believe that He could create something that we would need the later when He created us? Would He create a creative being without creating those things necessary for the creative being to use to create with?

In Hebrews 11:3 (KJV) *"Through faith we understand that the worlds were framed by the word of God, so that things which are seen were not made of things which do appear."*

It takes faith to understand the creative mentality of God. If you do not possess faith, you cannot begin to fathom how He uses His voice to do His framework. Hear this in your Spirit man. The worlds, plural, were framed by the Word of God. The interpretation of that passage takes in not only other planets, but all other dispensations and ages. In each of those "framed" worlds would be distinctive materials which would designate them as appearing in that distinctive framework. There was a man in England whose prophetic insights spurned the statement "all things are parallel". Now put this in your Spirit man. In the natural there are times when there are awesome advances on many fronts. But it must be stated that if this statement is true that all things are parallel, then there would be awesome advances in the realm of the spiritual at the same time as those taking place in the natural.

Now, let us move on to the next part of the verse, "The things which were seen were not made of things which do appear." It is a must that you realize the power of this text. The matter, or material used to make the things which were not seen were invisible. How is this to be? It is truly simple. If He is creating out of Himself then the material, or matter He uses, comes out of that invisible part of Him. He knows it is there, but He does not need to make a stack of material and then assemble them. He pre-designs and produces a manifestation which is a reflection of something already existing in the eternal past, and yet, it is visible now.

There is an old story which tells of a young man who was in a boxing match. He was taking a great deal of punches and when it came to the last round his manager told him he was losing the fight, and it was time that he reached way down inside himself and pull up that knockout punch. The young man roared out of the corner at the bell, and astonished the entire arena by knocking his opponent out cold and winning the bout. When asked how he did this after all the rounds he had supposedly lost he replied, " I just reached way down into myself and found that one punch that I knew would lay him out on the canvas." Each time God reached inside Himself, he drew out something never before seen or heard of. It was something which was distinctly God.

****

"Matter must obey our commands."

****

God made man in His own image. That means we have the power over matter. Matter must obey our commands. Why? Because we are made superior to the matter. This is not mind over matter we are addressing here. We are talking about the authority of the being God created in His image. It was the design that man and woman have dominion over the earth. That meant everything. Dominion over the plant world, the terra firma, the animal kingdom and anything else that had been created, or made, by God. Man was to be in authority, to dominate the environment. Until Adam and Eve sinned, they did exactly that. They ruled with God in the things He created and made.

God took the dust of the earth, which was His pre-designed matter which came out of His invisible self and formed man. Then He breathed the breath of life, which was also something which was inside Him, into man. Man stood up in a glorified state, not because that was his choice, but because it was His design. Imagine the first instant Adam stared into the face of God, the first words out of his mouth to His Creator. What did He say? What was his reaction? The Word states that we are created for His pleasure. That word always indicates worship. I cannot imagine Adam not bowing before Him and worshiping Him. He had His mind in him, so Adam intrinsically knew what was expected of the created. How else would he know how the animals were to be named and how they would respond? How else would he know how to tend to the garden God had given him dominion over? The Mind of God! Imagine talking to him face to face and not dying! Adam and Eve walked with Him every day when it became cool. Do you not wonder why God waited until it was cool? That meant that the sun was setting and that the process of pollination and reproduction which happens in the light of day was coming to rest. The bees were not buzzing around from flower to flower, the cattle on the thousand hillsides had eaten their fill, the lamb and the lion rested together in peace at days end. The evening was for the earth, and the earth began to rest with Him. All of creation would watch as God, Adam and Eve walked through the garden observing the growth of those things around them. Can you not see them as they reach out and touch the head of the tiger, the scales of the rhinoceros, the soft down on the fowls of the air. All of creation would worship the Creator as he walked by. They did not worship Adam and Eve, because they too were caught up in the symphony of praise to the One who had called them all out of Himself into the now.

Then, one simple conversation brought it all tumbling down. One Anti-God thought. One question would create such an upheaval that everything He had created would feel the impact of that one conversation from that time forward. The dream to have fellowship with His creations would be tainted by one simple act of disobedience. One animal was not acting like all the others. This one seemed to be different. It seemed that he had lost his desire to worship the Creator. The serpent had somehow learned the art of beguilement. The tree of the Knowledge of Good and Evil was forbidden for Adam and Eve to partake of. Why? Because it was a part of Him that He did not want them to experience. He did not want them to have to carry the weight of that knowledge in them. God knew what that knowledge would do to them. It would age them, make them weary, have pain and suffering. He knew how to have dominion over it because it was part of His knowledge. Yet, with all that was around them, they wanted more. They wanted to be equal. It seemed logical. They were so much like Him as it was. Why not have the same knowledge?

Then came the decree of banishment. Never again would they enter the garden. No longer would they talk with Him. The dream was over. The nightmare started. Childbirth became a laboring nine month ordeal. Each time Adam would dig into the earth he would sweat and grow weak. Where love once reigned, hate was present. The sun seemed hotter and the nights turned from cool to cold. All because of the thirst for knowledge.

****

"The spiritual holds matter together!"

****

Can you not see that this relationship, which He created in the beginning, is the same one He will reinstate when He comes for His Bride? He wants to walk with man and woman in the cool of the day once again. He wants what was. Some theologians have argued if God was all powerful, why not just make a creation which did not have the capacity to choose allegiance or love? I personally think that is one of the most ignorant concepts I have ever heard. The logical rationale is so diminished in that argument. He had already created that scenario. Just look around His throne. The living creatures are made for the distinct purpose indicated in the Word. They continually fulfill their design.

God wanted, and still does, a relationship with those who would love Him, as He loved them. Simple and uncomplicated. God creates man and woman with a mind, will and emotions in a glorified body with the option of choosing to be obedient or disobedient. When temptation came along, they both chose to eat of the tree of the Knowledge of Good and Evil. Let's emphasis the word "knowledge".

The spiritual holds matter together! The Lord gave me this awesome revelation a few days ago. When the Lord said this to me, I understood why miracles are going to explode all over.

He said, *"The spiritual holds the matter together. In the realm of the spirit, matter changes, because it no longer has anything to support it."*

When a gardener decides to uproot a plant, or tree, that has been in the ground for a great while, there is always the consideration of the root system. If he plans on replanting the plant, the gardener will remove as much of the environmental soil as is possible to make certain the plant will not go into shock when replanted. If the plant is just going to be removed and discarded the gardener simply pulls at the bottom of the plant and removes as much of the root system he can. If he truly wants those broken off roots to not regrow, he will then have to insert an agent to kill the roots. Even then, there is no way he can be certain he got them all. Only when the spring comes the next year will he be able to discern if the roots system was truly destroyed.

All too often in spiritual situations where we are removing a root system of indoctrinated unbelief, religion, denomination, theoretical theology or perverse ideology, it takes a while to truly discern the condition of the removal. Here is where faith must stand strong in the face of the taunt of the enemy. While the Adamic nature will say it is still in rulership, the spirit man must rise up in the power of its position in Christ and declare the thing dead. Believing is one thing, while declaring is another. There is power in declaration. In some cases, declaration must be made often to remind the Adamic nature of its defeat.

As you have been reading this book, God has been dealing with many roots in your belief system. He has called on you to remove many of these deathly roots in order for you to accomplish His divine plan for your life. Painful as it may seem at the time, this is precisely what you must do to become victorious. As you close the pages on this book, many will be tempted to dismiss the contents and walk away from the correction it has started in you. I plead with you, in the name of Jesus Christ, do not do that! You have been seeking a new and fresh walk with Him. You have said there must be more to the Kingdom of Heaven and as you have read through these pages you have found the key to that abundance in Him. Do not be as Lot's wife and look back. Set your face toward the Heavens, toward the Glory of God and breath in the fresh wind of His Spirit. Let it saturate your very being. Remember, He has planted you into new soil. There is no fear of spiritual shock ahead. He is waiting on you to grow into the Bride He is seeking. Remove the blemish, the spot. Remove the wrinkle from your garments, wash them white in His blood, and prepare to meet your Bridegroom. He is waiting for you. Grow!

"Heavenly Father, we declare the roots cut from addictive behaviors, from spirits of infirmities, from everything that tries to exalt itself against the knowledge of the Glory of God. We lay the axe to the root of the problem and we declare, "No root, no fruit." We choose to walk into the greater realm of God. We say we are free

to live in the greater miracle realm by the Spirit, and the word agrees that whom the Son sets free is free indeed, in Jesus' name. Amen!"

Renny McLean

CHAPTER TWENTY

Revival and Harvest

*"Revival cannot be organized, but we can set our sails
to catch the wind from Heaven when God chooses to blow
upon His people once again"*
-G. Campbell Morgan

Knowing the difference between revival and harvest will change your world. We must discern the difference between harvest mode and revival mode. Revival is the place of empowerment. But you don't live in the upper room; you have to go out and reap the harvest. If we do not go out and take the harvest, then the upper room experience is in vain. We don't realize that we are anointed and appointed to shake the world, not with theory, doctrine, or mental reasoning, but with signs and wonders and miracles. Then our upper room experience is not in vain. Forgive my boldness, but let's be honest. Some of us have been in the upper room experience for years, but we missed the harvest, and our families are going to hell. We just keep going and we think it's going to happen. I have news for you. Jesus is coming, not for a church in revival mode, but a church in harvest mode. Now is the hour God is raising up laborers. I am a laborer. The dilemma in the church is that we look to those who labor and wind up not laboring ourselves. God has called and appointed you for now. Based on that, let me make this statement again, "There is nothing right now, no matter what country you are from, that is void of divine significance." He is moving in harvest, and we must be sensitive to what the Spirit is saying.

Knowing God is doing it! God speaks to us by thoughts. How many of you have had that experience when all of a sudden, you're thinking gets canceled and something you weren't thinking of— something unimaginable—just comes in?

It's like suddenly you conceive the thoughts of God. He put this in my spirit just before the century turned.

The Lord said, *"There is a greater miracle realm out there."* I said, *"Lord I know that."* He said, *"The greatest manifestation of miracles will not be seen in Pentecost as you have known it."*

I said, "Lord, I don't understand. Why?" Then He told me we've come to the stage where we know how to box it in. We know how to make it work, package it, and when God comes in and does something new, we don't even realize we've become controlling. It can actually block what God is about to do.

I understood instantly. When revival first hits a church, it disturbs the atmosphere of the church. Until that atmosphere is broken, revival can't abide in the church. It will radically change the atmosphere of the church and create a hunger for something fresh and new.

The Lord said to me, *"The greatest miracles that are about to happen will not happen by conventional means. They will not be by conventional people, as you have known. This move I am doing on the earth will not have a reference point, like the faith movement had a reference point. What I am doing on the earth before I return will not need a reference point. The only reference will be the throne."*

The greater is about to explode! None of us know what is about to break out on the earth. Eye has not seen it, nor ear heard it . . . it hasn't even entered into our heart yet the things that God is about to do on the earth...

> *"But as it is written, Eye hath not seen, nor ear heard, neither have entered into the heart of man, the things which God hath prepared for them that love him.* (1 Corinthians 2:9)

You think the supernatural manifestation of unusual signs and wonders is something but the greater is about to come. The greater is hovering over the church and it's starting to unravel, and you are going to see it. God is about to explode in a demonstration of signs and wonders that will leave the church speechless. We haven't seen anything yet. There has never been a time like now where the Heavens or spirit world is so aligned with the earth as it is now. You can smell it in the very atmosphere. There is an expectancy in the air that corresponds to the Heavens for what God wants to do on the earth. We are on the cutting edge of it.

We are in overtime! As we broke into January 2001, the Lord showed me seals over the church. One of them is finances. One is creative miracles, and one is revelation knowledge. I'm seeing the plan and cycle of God. This is so different from any other time because now we are in overtime. That's why no one can tell you what is going to happen. We are in overtime. You ask me why? We have almost fulfilled the days according to time. Things are being revealed now. That's why the Bible uses the word dispensation, meaning "a revealed period of time."

Knowing the supernatural acts of God is a must for the vessels set in the Glory! The only way we are going to know what is happening on the earth now is by revelation. You're coming to a place where you listen to the prophetic voice, as you never have before.

The Bible says in Amos 3:7 (KJV), *"Surely the Lord GOD will do nothing, but he revealeth his secret unto his servants the prophets."*

If there is an hour when prophets are going to dream, if there is ever an hour when prophets are going to see visions, if there is an hour when prophets are going to have their angels visit them and tell them what is about to come, we are living in that hour.

Just after the fall things were so aligned to the earth. The Spirit world started to walk among men. Now is the hour when angels will begin to come into your churches and sit down with you. You'll have a spirit here and a spirit there. Just know there are angels dispatched for this period of time to help the church to bring in the harvest. This is no time to play games. This is no time for business as usual. This is the hour the church will have her act together. I believe there will be city-wide miracles. I believe there will be statewide miracles. Miracles will literally shake a city and a state. I believe one miracle will bring government officials to their knees calling for an explanation of this move of God. God will hold nothing back in this hour!

****

"The prophetic will be different from what we've known."

****

The Holy Spirit is the reference point. The devil is delivering everything in his arsenal to the church. Do you really think that it is the plan of God to withhold everything from the church? What you have prayed for, what you have prophesied? If we stay in what God has called us to do, we will be partakers of the signs and the wonders the earth has never known before. Some things that are happening right now we can't speak about, because no one will be an authority on the subject. Do you know who the ultimate authority is? The Holy Ghost! That's why He is going to be the reference point for everything that happens on the earth. Our knowing is by revelation!

The Lord said to me, *"Intelligence is going to be revelatory but the vocabulary will be prophetic. The prophetic will be different from what we've known."* When I asked Him how it would be different He said, *"Too long My servants have set the tide. The moment it comes out of their mouth, it is on the earth. You are subconsciously looking for it in the future but you don't have to look in the future for your missing arm. You don't have to look in the future for missing eyeballs. You don't have to look in the future for new body parts. It is here and now! It is here and now!"*

How can we put something in a timeframe that isn't even guaranteed? The only thing that is guaranteed is here and now— not tomorrow, not next year. We are trained subconsciously to look for something way over yonder that is hovering over the earth. God wants us to be bold enough to reach out and take it now.

Millennium intelligence will be revelatory! There are manifestations dispatched from the throne, hovering over the earth as you read this. We are not pressing into them. Millennium intelligence will be revelatory, but the vocabulary will be prophetic. This is why, at times, we don't speak to make something happen now. We are speaking things as they are happening. If you believe something has happened, you're supposed to act like it. You're supposed to praise. You're not supposed to act as though this thing is still coming. It's HERE and NOW . . . that new dimension of faith.

I see a new dimension of faith coming into the church—a faith the church has never known before—a faith that is being seen here and now. You're going to understand what Jesus meant when He said, "I only do what I hear and what I see."

"Then answered Jesus and said unto them, Verily, verily, I say unto you, The Son can do nothing of himself, but what he seeth the Father do: for what things soever he doeth, these also doeth the Son likewise. For the

Father loveth the Son, and sheweth him all things that himself doeth: and he will shew him greater works than these, that ye may marvel." (John 5:19-20)

Now you can understand why the intelligence has to be revelatory. If you see it, it exists and if you call it, it is framed. Some of us right now are high on vision but we are low on framing it. It's there and until you declare what you see, it stays out there. It can stay out there for another ten, twenty, thirty, forty, fifty years until someone decides to declare it.

There are some things the church has never seen. There are new manifestations coming on the earth. There is a new dimension coming in the church. That's why you can't sit still in church. God has put a new expectation in your spirit. Can you honestly say that you have an expectation of the new in signs, wonders and miracles? You know why you never had the expectation before? Because you didn't quite see how it was possible. Now you can see it is and your expectation is rising.

I will never forget the meeting I had in England, in a place named Watford. I was asked to preach for three consecutive nights at a Church of God.

God said to me, *"You will not preach one word."* I asked, *"Why?" "The people have not come to hear a sermon; they have come to see a sermon. You will sit down and not speak one word and I will heal the whole church."*

I clearly remember sitting down in that meeting and I remember my wife, Marina, looking at me as if to say, "Take the microphone, Renny. People are beginning to get nervous."

Then the Lord said this to my spirit.

"Manifestations are to be invited. When they are invited, then they have to be entertained. If you don't step into it, you'll find the manifestation lifts." The Lord said, *"Have them worship."*

As we were worshiping the Lord, I saw a cloud come over the meeting and it covered the entire sanctuary. Everyone was worshiping. People in wheelchairs stood up—healed. Bones formed and not a prayer was prayed. Eardrums formed; legs grew out four to five inches, just by being in the presence of the Lord.

The Lord said to me, *"Worship is an affirmation of Me being present. That's why when I am affirmed I have to manifest Myself."*

I sat down and wheel chairs came up one by one. Hearing aids came up. The platform was filled with hearing aids, glasses, canes and crutches. This is what the people said, "When you stood and said, 'The Lord is going to minister,' we knew it could only be God, the way it all happened." I clearly remember that my speech left me and I took my seat. As I sat, the cloud of the Lord came over the congregation. They saw Jesus sitting next to me. He got up and stood before them with His hands raised and people audibly heard Him say, "Rise and be thou healed."

The total congregation stood up and was healed. There was a woman there with twenty-two diseases in her body. She stood up when she saw Jesus stand up and say, "Rise and be thou healed." Later, when she went to the doctor, the test results showed all twenty-two diseases had vanished. The doctors were reporting that cancers were being healed. Twenty-eight cases were healed in one night and not a prayer was prayed. When I went back to my hotel room, the Lord said to me, "Would you like to see that again?" I said, "Lord, I would like to see more than that."

He said, *"Down through the ages I have given every man and woman a foretaste of the realm that is going to be on the earth, and this is one of them."*

People want to know if Jesus is in the house. We are approaching a time where we are not concerned whether we hear a message. Our concern is whether or not Jesus in the house.

He said further, *"There will no longer be personalities of man. It's going to be the personality of Me in the house. Signs and wonders and miracles will be the norm, but My people will come out of personalities. And they will come into Me."*

I don't care if anyone lays hands on me. Today, most of us look to an earthly being to affirm us, so we don't step into God's presence for ourselves. The fact that you step into His presence means that you are affirmed. Man was thrown from that presence in Adam's fall. The fact that we stand before His presence, and we have access to see Him as He is should be affirmation enough. We couldn't want a greater validation than that from the King of kings and Lord of lords. We are going to have services where angelic beings will walk into the services and escort Jesus into the worship service. I can see it even as I'm saying it here.

Praise releases angelic visitations, paving the way for more angelic beings to enter into the services. There are glories coming into meetings and we won't know how to contain it. All we can do is stand there with unveiled faces, beholding the word as a mirror, and we'll be transformed from one Glory to another. We won't be able to pitch tents in past glories. This is the reason why every past Glory is overshadowed by the presence of the new. The new always carries a higher awareness than the previous realm. Until you are in the new realm, you don't know it. It's not something you can study. It's something you have to experience. Until you do, you won't know it. Experience will do something for you that nothing else will do.

The mysteries of God are spoken in codes. I want you to notice how Paul said it in 1 Corinthians 2:7:

> *"But we speak the wisdom of God in a mystery, even the hidden wisdom, which God ordained before the world unto our glory."*

Let me paraphrase it another way. If there is ever an hour the codes are being revealed it's now. I'm talking about the things in the Spirit that are indeed coded. That's why sometimes when someone speaks you may hear something they didn't even know they're saying. It is the answer to your prayer. It's the answer to your situation and it was coded. The person didn't know they were speaking it. I am going to say this in the realm of the Spirit. Revelation precedes manifestation! There are manifestations of the Spirit that are coded. They don't happen for the sake of happening. They are divinely coded. Jesus was an enemy of Pharisees because He alone knew the code. In the Hebraic, it conveys the idea that anyone who moves in signs, wonders and miracles cannot walk without divine (not the norm) revelation. There is no way you can have revelation without having signs and wonders. It's impossible. There is no revelation without having a manifestation. The manifestation confirms the revelation came from God. That's why the Pharisees looked at Jesus and said, "We know you come from God because of the things you are saying, because nobody else is saying them. Nobody else knows them." Jesus spoke in code.

Many of you have said something in a meeting and it released a whole new wave of God. Do you ever notice we say the phrase, "Was it something I said?" Oh, yes, it is. There are times in the healing ministry when something comes out of you, and you know you must stop preaching because the healing presence is there. It was in something you said. As Jesus was teaching, the power of God was present to heal. Do you know why the devil hates revelation knowledge?

Because the Bible says, "My people are destroyed for lack of knowledge: because thou hast rejected knowledge, I will also reject thee." Hosea 4:6 (KJV)

****

"Intellectualism has become the means by which we determine our reality."

****

Why people don't want revelation knowledge is beyond me. Without it there is no empowerment.

In the natural, we get trapped in mental reasoning. I clearly remember the Lord putting this in my spirit: "Intellectualism has become the means by which we determine our reality." I believe this is how we get stifled in the realm of the Spirit. No wonder the Bible says you have to renew your mind.

"And be not conformed to this world: but be ye transformed by the renewing of your mind, that ye may prove what is that good, and acceptable, and perfect, will of God." (Romans 12:2)

What is going to happen is beyond mental reasoning and beyond your doctrine because there is no doctrine pointing toward what is to be.

I'll tell you who is going to be the reference point. It's the Holy Ghost. As that starts to happen, and it becomes the norm you will find your intellect waning. You're going to find that it's easier and easier to step in and out of the realm of the Spirit. You're going to know how to go in and out unhindered. You'll go into eternity and bring something from eternity back into time. Your head won't get in the way of it. Intellectualism has become the means by which we determine what is real. If we lived back in the days when the axe head swung, folks would say it was witchcraft. Who said God couldn't make an axe head swing or a donkey talk? I do know who says it; your doctrine and by laws. In our indoctrination is an intellect that denies extreme spiritual manifestations. We say, "How can this be God?" Brethren, I don't know how He parted the Red Sea. I don't know if He stuck His tongue out, put His foot down or put His hand up. All I know is He made the Red Sea part. We must come to the place where we don't care how we get healed or delivered, provided we get it God's way.

If there is ever an hour when God is going to give visions about His manifestations, it is now. We must pick up on the things God is showing us. When He shows them, we have got to call them forth, and when we start calling them forth, they will start happening. The problem with a lot of us is that we sit down waiting for it to happen. The intelligence of the millennium is the revelatory. This is where the old conflicts with the new.

First, second, and third day comprehension will remap your mind. We are third day people stuck with our first day comprehension. We are still in infancy. This is how it works; if I do anything a little different from you, you get offended. We don't have second day comprehension where we anoint a man or a woman as God wills. He will use them as He wills. Paul said, "When I was a child (first day comprehension), I acted like a child. But when I became a man, I put away childish things. You know what first day comprehension caused us to do? Label people. This move of God has no denominational boundaries. It is not Pentecostal. It is not Baptist. It is not Methodist or Presbyterian. First day comprehension educated you in differences and isms. That's why when God brings in a new voice the church can't handle it, because the new are more spiritual than those who have been there for years. Those who come in fresh through the door have less religion to work through.

God is going to raise people who are not necessarily known. That's the generation I'm looking for. I am not seeking after a generation who knows how to be cute, or how to dot their "i's" and cross their "t's". There is a remnant group of people who know the throne of God. I'm fed up with hearing about the need for good doctrine. You see, revival broke the first day comprehension mode. In the upper room they thought this thing that was happening was Jewish. This move of God goes far beyond liturgical, or Pentecostal, denominational lines. You know what first day comprehension did? It taught us to be judgmental. Those of you who have traveled the world know this is true. We must change our mindset. There is a challenge facing us in these last days. The challenge is to overcome the eight percent intellect of the Adamic mentality and stimulate the eternal mind of Christ.

My Dear Friends

I wanted to take this final moment to share something from my heart. Words cannot express the gratitude and thankfulness in my heart for all the wonderful expressions of love our family has experienced over the last few years. The awesome testimonies from people all over the world who have been impacted by the revelations in this book have caused my heart to rejoice.

You may have just arrived at the end of this book, but the true journey into the heavens has just become. You now know that time has fallen. You are more aware of the power of His NOW than ever before. How exciting it must be to know that you have just stepped out of the mundane world of religion and into the everlasting supernatural realm of the creator of the universe. Never again will you be satisfied with the status quo of mediocrity. You are in a new day, a third day awareness that something exciting is just around the bend.

As you plan your calendar for this year, do not fail to make plans to attend one of our summits in an area near you. Our International Summit in Texas is filled with leaders from around the world. The level of worship is unprecedented, the level of revelation is off the chart, and the friends you make are eternal! You must make plans to come. I would love to meet you personally and shake your hand and tell you how much I appreciate your prayers and support.

On behalf of myself, Marina, Maranatha, Caleb and Zoe, it is our prayer that you will continue in the glory of God each and every day of your life until He returns. Remember, we go from Glory to Glory! Praise-A-Lujah!"

Dr. R. G. McLean
Global Glory, Inc.
www.globalglory.org

Renny McLean is available for speaking engagements and personal appearances. For more information send an email to: mm76051@aol.com, or send a request to the publisher at: info@advbooks.com

To order additional copies of this book or to see a complete list of books that we publish, visit our online bookstore at: www.advbookstore.com

*A*dvantage
BOOKS

Longwood, Florida, USA
"we bring dreams to life"™
www.advbooks.com

www.ingramcontent.com/pod-product-compliance
Lightning Source LLC
Chambersburg PA
CBHW020354100426
42812CB00001B/54